Istanbul Eats
Exploring the Culinary Backstreets

Ansel Mullins & Yigal Schleifer

ℋBOYUT

Istanbul Eats
Exploring the Culinary
Backstreets

ISBN 978-975-23-0720-9

Certificate Number: 10855

AUTHORS
Ansel MULLINS
Yigal SCHLEIFER

EDITOR
Vanessa H. LARSON

GENERAL DIRECTOR
Bülent ÖZÜKAN

GENERAL MANAGER
Nilgün ÖZÜKAN

CREATIVE DIRECTOR
Murat ÖNEŞ

COVER ART
Selçuk ARIKAN

© **Boyut Publishing & Co.**

Koza Plaza A Blok 26th Floor Tekstilkent
34235, Esenler- İSTANBUL
Phone: (0212) 413 33 33
Fax: (0212) 413 33 34

Text and photographs © 2010
Ansel Mullins and Yigal Schleifer

PRINTING

BOYUT MATBAACILIK A.Ş.
Matbaacılar Sitesi, 1. Cadde,
No. 115 34204 Bağcılar- İSTANBUL
Phone: (0212) 413 33 33
Fax: (0212) 413 33 34

www.boyutstore.com
e-mail: info@boyut.com.tr

4th Edition: 2013 April, Istanbul

Cultural Products Hotline
+90 212 444 53 53

You can obtain this book and for all other
products from above phone number without
paying any shipment fee.

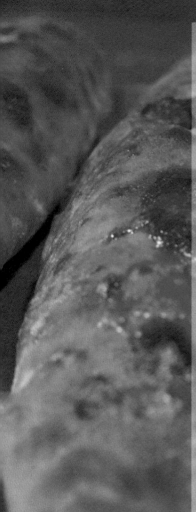

Introduction

This book got its start, naturally, over lunch, when we asked ourselves a simple question: Why are small, traditional eateries—where some of the best meals in Istanbul await—so often overlooked? Why, in a city with such rich culinary backstreets, are these areas and their bounty of good food so rarely explored and celebrated?

In response, we launched Istanbuleats.com, a website devoted to collecting the best undiscovered local eateries you might not always find on your own. We're talking serious food for serious eaters, hold the frills.

Beyond the kebab—and what you will find listed in most guidebooks—lies a wide range of unique Turkish regional cuisines and restaurants with hints of Balkan, Caucasian and Middle Eastern cooking. With this book as your trusty guide to the culinary backstreets of Istanbul, you will know what to eat and where to eat it.

Because prices tend to fluctuate in Turkey, we have decided not to include them in our reviews. Most of the spots covered vary from very inexpensive to modest. More importantly, we consider all of our selections high in value. Alcohol is generally not among the offerings, unless otherwise indicated in the review or in the index (p.172). In general, we recommend making reservations for dinner.

Welcome to Istanbul's Culinary Backstreets, *afiyet olsun!*

Ansel & Yigal
Founders, Istanbuleats.com

Table of Contents

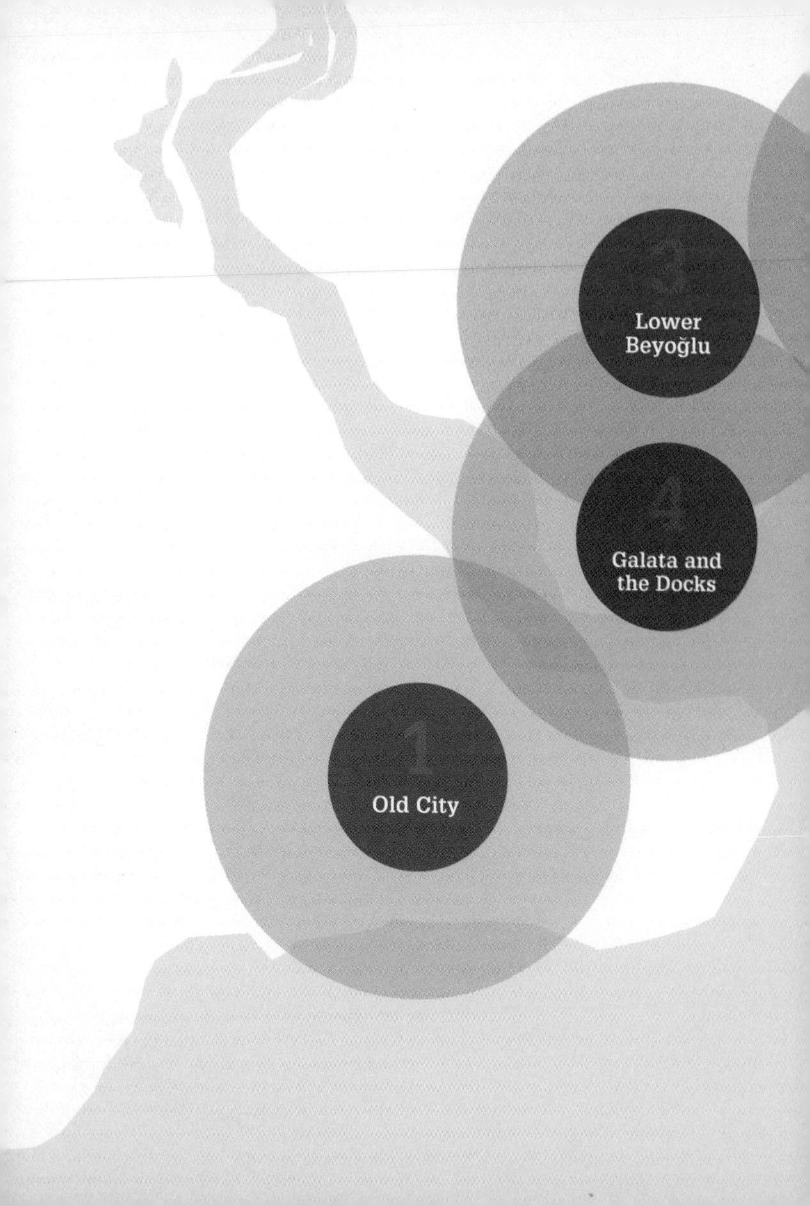
3
Lower Beyoğlu
4
Galata and the Docks
1
Old City

Upper Beyoğlu

Bosphorus

Asian Side and Islands

Old City

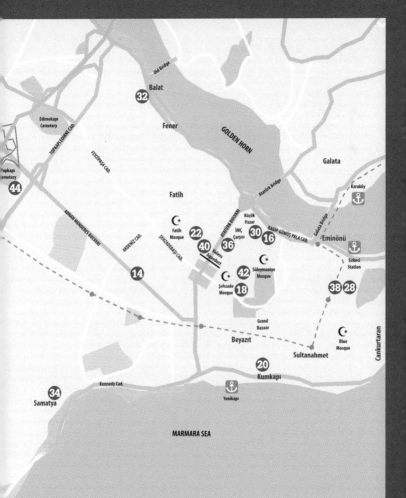

Balat
32

Fener

GOLDEN HORN

Galata

Edirnekapı
Cemetery

Topkapı
Cemetery
44

Karaköy

TOPKAPI EDIRNE CAD.

JEVDİPAŞA CAD.

Fatih

Atatürk Bridge

RAGIP GÜMÜŞ PALA CAD.

Galata Bridge

Eminönü

ADNAN MENDERES BULVARI

AKDENİZ CAD.

ŞEHZADEBAŞI CAD.

Fatih
Mosque
22

ATATÜRK BULVARI

Küçük
Pazar

İMÇ
Çarşısı
36

30

16

40

Valens
Aqueduct

Sirkeci
Station

14

Şehzade
Mosque
18

42

Süleymaniye
Mosque

38 28

Grand
Bazaar

Beyazıt

Blue
Mosque

Sultanahmet

Cankurtaran

20

Kumkapı

Kennedy Cad.

Yenikapı

34
Samatya

MARMARA SEA

Tram   Highway   Main Road   Mosque   Ferry

Akdeniz Hatay Sofrası

Old City

Ahmediye Caddesi 44/A,
Fatih
212 531 3333
8:30am-11:30pm

THE SYRIAN CONNECTION

Turkey's southernmost province, Hatay, was in fact part of Syria until the 1930s, and its food is closer in spirit and flavor to what's found on menus in Aleppo or Damascus. This restaurant is run by a family from Hatay and does brisk business serving up authentic and very good food from the region.

Hatay's Syrian roots are especially obvious when it comes to starters, of which the stars are a creamy hummus–an item surprisingly hard to find in Istanbul–and Mütebbel, a smoky eggplant and yogurt salad. Two zesty salads tossed with tart pomegranate molasses, one made with cracked green olives and another with za-'atar, a wild herb that tastes something like fresh oregano, are also excellent.

The extensive main course menu has several kinds of kebabs and a rotating lineup of daily specials, mostly home-style soups, stews and savory tarts. But the real show-stopping dishes are Tuzda Tavuk and Tuzda Kuzu, chicken or lamb stuffed with rice and baked in salt, which need to be ordered at least two and a half hours in advance. Entombed inside a dome of rock salt, the meat is slow-cooked in a wood-burning oven, then wheeled out to your table on a cart. A waiter douses the dome with a clear flammable liquid while another lights it and runs away as the salt erupts in a massive burst of fire that would be the basis of a lawsuit in most other countries, but here is all part of the fun.

Once the flames have died down, the waiter returns with a mallet and an industrial-sized chisel and cracks open the salt to reveal steaming, succulent meat (and, in the case of the chicken, deliciously crispy skin).

If you still have room left for dessert, try the excellent Künefe, a traditional Middle Eastern sweet made out of a mozzarella-like cheese sandwiched between layers of crispy shredded wheat and doused with a sugary syrup. ◆

Kibleçeşme Caddesi 96, Kantarcılar
(Küçük Pazarı), Eminönü
212 522 5909
8:30am-7pm

Altan Şekerleme

MORE THAN JUST EYE CANDY

From the potpourri of run-down yet extremely photogenic shops in Küçük Pazarı, one storefront beckons from a distance. The front window is stacked with psychedelic pyramids of Turkish delight, or lokum, laid out into long white rows that are impossibly pink or deep amber on the inside. Welcome to the dreamy, sugar-dusted world of Altan Şekerleme–or, better yet, Candyland.

With its aged marble-topped counters and worn wooden cabinets, the shop bears a nostalgic patina strangely absent in this ancient city. Unlike so many places that make sad attempts at recreating "Old Istanbul," Altan is an effortless standard-bearer of late Ottoman authenticity. That's probably because the secret recipes, the store, the production floor upstairs and all its trappings have been passed down from father to son for four generations since 1865. "For us, this is not just a candy business. It's a family tradition, and an Ottoman tradition,

we are working at," says 86-year-old Abdullah Altanoğlu, who now owns the shop. The gül (rosewater) Turkish delight is an almost sensual experience, while the sakızlı (mastic gum-flavored) lokum is interesting as a novelty. But the pistachio-filled fıstıklı lokum is a showstopper.

The sublime, almost gummy confection surrounding the crunchy nut core would convince even the most committed chocoholic to buy a box of the stuff.

Altan also prides itself on its tahin helvası–a sweet paste of crushed sesame seeds studded with pine nuts–and its wide variety of akide, Turkish rock candies, which sit in handsome glass jars on the countertop.

As surely as the Altanoğlu family will pass the keys to another generation to guard its centuries-old secrets, their sweet sugar-dusted lokum will remain not only a Turkish but–we hope and pray–global delight. ◆

Dedeefendi Caddesi 4,
Eminönü
212 512 6406
9am-9pm

Doğu Türkistan Vakfı Aş Evi

EAST MEETS EAST

With the particularly un-catchy name of Doğu Türkistan Vakfı Aş Evi (or East Turkistan Foundation Food House–DTVAE from here on), it's clear this restaurant is not aiming for mass-market appeal. Located inside the pleasant courtyard of a 16th-century former medrese (religious school), DTVAE serves up hearty dishes for homesick Uighurs, a Muslim Turkic people who hail from western China's Xinjiang province, or "East Turkistan," as it is known in Turkey.

Turks and Uighurs share a linguistic and culinary bond, with Uighur cooking perhaps providing a blueprint of the "original" Turkish cooking. Whereas the classic Turkish kitchen reflects a mix of various regional influences and the highfalutin tastes of the Ottoman court, Uighur cooking retains the simplicity of what were originally a nomadic people. It's so simple, in fact, that DTVAE's menu is basically limited to three items–two of which are different takes on mantı, the traditional Turkish dumpling.

The restaurant's centerpiece dish is Lagman, a staple of Uighur cooking made from handmade noodles, somewhat resembling udon noodles, that are boiled and served with a stir-fry of beef, onions and green peppers. The mantı, topped with yogurt and red pepper flakes, is delicious, putting to shame most of the other versions found around town (which seem to favor dough over filling).

The restaurant's other mantı dish–a much larger dough pocket stuffed with a meat/onion mixture that reminded us of a Chinese soup dumpling–is also very nice, especially when eaten with a schmear of the oily red pepper paste from a jar on the table.

DTVAE has a few outside tables, where you can eat under the shade of three massive maple trees, and a handful of tables inside. A visit to this peaceful oasis will transport you to East Turkistan. ◆

Ördekli Bakkal Sokak 10,
Kumkapı
212 458 2637
7am-8pm

Doyuran

WORKING-CLASS HERO

We usually steer clear of the touristy old district of Kumkapı, where you're more likely to be accosted by aggressive maitre d's from over-priced fish restaurants than to find something simple, tasty and reasonably priced to eat. But tucked into Kumkapı's back streets are a few hidden dining gems that locals in the know frequent. At Doyuran Lokantası, the men at the next table may be wearing spackle-crusted work shirts and have measuring tapes on their belts, but they know their food. In most Istanbul neighborhoods, the working class sets the culinary bar, and they set it high. They want it fast, fresh, cheap and as close as possible to their mothers' recipes. Offering up four or five daily lunch specials, including mantı (home-made Turkish dumplings), chickpeas over rice, and various traditional stews, Doyuran's husband and wife team answers the working man's call with ease, the service both professional and homey. In order to try several of the day's specials, ask for small portions, or "az."

"Bismillah," said owner-operator Musa Ergenç, invoking the name of God as he cut the first piece of steaming Musaka (mousaka) from a large pan. And heavenly it was, the eggplant richly saturated but not too oily. Unlike the Greek version, which is usually topped with béchamel sauce, the top layer of Doyuran's consists of a refreshing blast of chopped tomatoes. Ispanak Yemeği, a steam table standard of stewed spinach and rice more associated with filling the belly than exciting the senses, here provoked a double take.

This didn't look or taste anything like the heavy, overcooked green mush we're accustomed to elsewhere. Instead, each flavor presented itself separately, from the fresh spinach to the light tomato sauce base.

A dollop of yogurt on the side left the dish with a cool finish. ◆

Atpazarı 11/A,
Fatih
212 533 4296
10am-12:30am

Eski Kafa

NEW-AGE OLD-FASHIONED

The Turkish phrase "eski kafa" means "old-fashioned to the hilt." Yet Eski Kafa, with its Zen lodge décor and signs boasting "all natural," "organic" and "no hormones," is in fact decidedly new age–to the hilt. This little eatery keeps a slow food agenda on the table, with traditional Turkish dishes prepared fresh with what's in season.

We recommend the Kuru Patlıcan Dolma appetizer, or dried eggplant stuffed with rice. As the boisterous chef explained: "Show me a fresh, natural, local eggplant after the season is over! There are none, so in the winter we use dried ones, like our grandmothers used to do." The stuffing was just spicy enough to elicit an arch of the eyebrows, while the dried eggplant casing had the strength to withstand fierce stuffing (unlike the limp skin of a fresh eggplant), resulting in a denser dolma that packed a wallop. Yüksük Çorbası, or "thimble soup," a specialty of Adana–a city in southern Turkey

known for its flavorful cuisine–came packed with homemade Turkish dumplings and chickpeas in a spicy broth.

For the main course we couldn't resist an order of the Gulaş, which the owner informed us was an original Turkish recipe of no direct relation to the more celebrated Hungarian goulash, but, at the same time, possibly its ancestor. Unlike the soupy Magyar variety, gulaş à la Turca was composed of ever-tender slow-roasted strips of beef seemingly dry-rubbed with spices and wrapped in bay leaves, its flavor quite intense and concentrated.

The original goulash or not? That's debatable. But this was definitely one of the better roast beef dishes we'd had in Istanbul.

Though their slow food credo and laid-back service might be more appreciated in upmarket neighborhoods elsewhere in Istanbul, there's a certain feng shui at Eski Kafa that we hope will never change. ◆

Sultanahmet Dining Secrets

Call it the Sultanahmet Squeeze: How to stay close to the monuments of the Old City yet avoid eating in tourist traps? We get asked this question a lot. Since the Sultanahmet area is primarily a tourism zone, locals-only haunts are few and far between. At most restaurants, prices tend to be higher than usual, while quality and service are unreliable, at best. That said, there are some fine places to eat in the area. We've compiled a short list of restaurants to help you avoid the traps.

AHIRKAPI BALIKÇISI

We found this little grilled fish and beer dive while popping out for a drink from a dry wedding at the lovely wooden dervish lodge, Dede Efendi. With a simple menu dominated by fresh seafood at reasonable prices, a smattering of rickety tables, and colorful locals sipping rakı, this is just the sort of place a concierge might tell you avoid.

In warm weather, when they drag a few tables out onto the sidewalk, there are few better places in Sultanahmet to eat a simple grilled fish washed down with a cold beer.

Keresteci Hakkı Sokak 46, Cankurtaran/Ahırkapı
212 518 4988
3pm-midnight

GİRİTLİ

Giritli deserves more ink than we can afford it here. This elegant yet comfortable fish restaurant, serving food typical of the Turks who once lived on the island of Crete, is full most nights with groups of locals and tourists taking advantage of a prix fixe menu that includes bottomless glasses of local wine, rakı or beer. But the food here more than holds its own. While the grilled octopus leg in olive oil is close to perfect, we get really worked up for the seafood and orzo salad and the olives stuffed with walnuts and feta–part of the dozen or so starters brought to the table. In the warm months Giritli's garden is just as pleasant any rooftop terrace.

**Keresteci Hakkı Sokak,
Cankurtaran/Ahırkapı
212 458 2270
noon-midnight**

TARİHİ SULTANAHMET KÖFTECİSİ

Tarihi Sultanahmet Köftecisi is the real deal for köfte, or meatballs. All those framed, hand-written letters from movie stars, politicians and military generals that cover the walls of this Sultanahmet mainstay are not complaints.

The restaurant's İnegöl-style köfte–that's the log format of the meatball, not the patty–is pleasantly springy, aromatic and juicy. When dressed with a spicy red pepper sauce (served upon request) and stuffed into a fresh hunk of bread, it borders on divine. We like to sit in the front room at the old marble tables to watch the action at the grill.

Divanyolu Caddesi 12, Sultanahmet
212 520 0566
11am-midnight

VONALI CELAL

Located on the coastal road that hugs Istanbul's ancient city walls, Vonalı Celal serves a wide range of homey and satisfying Black Sea dishes, with fresh bread baked in its brick oven. The restaurant offers a prix fixe menu that offers five courses–one of which is devoted to all things pickled, including green plums and cherries–and some 20-plus dishes. Price-wise, it's a fairly good deal, although we opted to go à la carte on our visit. Highlights included Çeşni, a dip made of tangy, crumbly white cheese and walnuts; cabbage leaves stuffed with rice; Yumurtalı Sakarca, a Spanish omelet-like egg dish that was stuffed with herbs and pearl onions; and Kaldırık, a wild green stewed in olive oil.

We also enjoyed the Kuymak (also called Muhlama), a kind of Black Sea fondue, made by mixing melted cheese and butter together with cornmeal, which gives the dish a surprisingly pleasant grittiness.

Kennedy Caddesi Sahil Yolu 40/1, Ahırkapı
212 516 1893
noon-midnight

Hocapaşa Sokak 22,
Sirkeci
212 519 3216
6am-11pm

Kasap Osman

A CURE FOR DÖNER FATIGUE

Though İskender Kebap is a registered trademark of the famous Kepapçı İskender restaurant in Bursa, in İstanbul imitations are ubiquitous. But unlike designer knock-offs in the Grand Bazaar, the "pirated" İskender Kebap at Kasap Osman ("Osman the Butcher" in Turkish) is most certainly the real thing, if not better.

Döner, slices of lamb stacked like pancakes on a tall skewer and slowly turned before a vertical grill, is the most important factor in any İskender Kebap. Though charcoal was traditionally used to roast the döner, these days gas and electric grills are common. Sadly, Kasap Osman recently yielded to this trend and moved to gas, although their döner remains expertly roasted.

Naturally, the quality of the meat plays an important role as well, and who better to trust at the spit than Osman, who actually is a former butcher. He and his team also have experience working in their favor, having turned a döner spit from the same corner every day for the last 25 years. Timed to coincide with the lunch-hour rush, at around noon the usta starts shaving off the first long ribbons of succulent döner.

The döner is sent to the kitchen, where it's turned into döner-based dishes. For İskender, the cooked meat is laid over a bed of chopped flatbread in a clay dish, garnished with peppers and tomatoes and dressed with a thin tomato sauce.

The dish is then quickly fired in the oven, crisping the saucy bread on the bottom and softening the garnish. Finally, the whole dish is doused with butter browned in a skillet and a quick dollop of thick yogurt is added to one side. We can often hear our İskender sizzling on its way to the table.

It's quite logical that someone trademarked so noble a kebab. But if you can't manage the official İskender Kebap pilgrimage to Bursa, head over to Kasap Osman for the best genuine fake İskender in the city. ◆

Kısmet Muhallebicisi

FUNKY CHICKEN

A li Bey, the owner of a cubby-sized restaurant called Kısmet, sounded a bit like Bubba Gump listing the menu: "We've got chicken soup, fried chicken gizzards, shredded chicken breast, dark chicken meat, chicken and rice, chicken with onions and peppers and, for something sweet, chicken breast pudding." There were other items on the menu, but Ali Bey was clearly pushing the chicken. Considering that we were in a pudding shop, the menu's concept became clear. Any self-respecting Turkish pudding man must serve Tavuk Göğsü–a pudding made out of chicken breast and milk–first and foremost. A man after our own heart, Ali Bey seems to have worked backward from dessert, filling in the rest of the menu with what was left over after the chicken breasts were rendered into pudding.

We started with the chicken soup. In Turkish, one does not "eat" soup; soup is "drunk"–an homage to the stock, presumably. At Kısmet the stock is superior: simple chicken broth, devoid of any thickening agents or, really, anything at all. This is down-to-the-bone, pure chicken soup–the soft shreds of chicken and thin noodles are merely the icing on the cake. As a main course, the gizzards, Taşlık, came sizzling in a skillet with chopped peppers and tomatoes.

The defining moment of the meal was the presentation of Ali Bey's chicken breast pudding. Beside the plate of thick, white pudding the waiter set a shaker of cinnamon. We take our pudding neat, however, and Ali Bey, watching from behind the counter, seemed to approve. Unlike fibrous chicken breast puddings we've had around town, this one was remarkably smooth and, in flavor, akin to a fine rice pudding.

After we paid our bill, Ali Bey asked if we enjoyed the pudding. "Of course," we replied, meeting eyes with a man who, like us, plans a meal around the dessert. ◆

Köfteci Arnavut

ON THE GOOD SHIP MEATBALL SHOP

Perhaps it's the proximity to the Golden Horn or the weathered wood interior, but we get a distinctly maritime feeling at Köfteci Arnavut, a tiny köfte joint. The members of the İştay family, who opened the place in 1947, run the place with ship-shape efficiency.

Ali, the 76-year-old father, constantly sweeps the floor and wipes down the Formica-topped tables, like a sailor dutifully swabbing the decks. Daughter Mine, meanwhile, issues clipped, urgent orders to the hustling grill master and waiters, as if she were the captain of a tanker navigating particularly treacherous waters.

In Turkey, grilled meatballs are serious business. Every Istanbul neighborhood has several small restaurants serving köfte, usually for a demanding lunch crowd. With so many köfte restaurants, how does one place distinguish itself from the others? In our experience, the truly winning places eschew the traditional köfte, which is log-shaped and slightly chewy, in favor of something more patty-like. Köfteci Arnavut's square-shaped köfte is very tasty and unusually thin, cooked on a charcoal grill until it's slightly crispy around the edges. The restaurant also serves Piyaz, the cold white bean salad that traditionally accompanies the meatballs, and a small assortment of soups and other dishes.

What also sets Köfteci Arnavut apart is its location, at the entrance to the historic Balat neighborhood, once a primarily Jewish and Greek enclave.

Its narrow streets are lined with small, Ottoman-era buildings, many of which have been renovated as part of a UNESCO project. Köfteci Arnavut, on the other hand, certainly looks like it could use some restoration of its own.

Still, as the top-notch köfte and the dedicated service show, the restaurant has set a course that needs little improvement. ◆

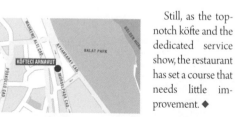

32

Küçük Ev

FANTASTIC VOYAGE

"Hamsi, one lira!" a fishmonger shouted from a rickety stand spread with glistening fresh fish. Judging by the cackles heard nearby, this man was a common source of amusement, a well-known village idiot. "I just sent a message to one of my customers to come and buy these fish for one lira. He replied that he's in America– imagine that!" he said, showing us his cell phone.

Unlike the fish markets of Beyoğlu and Kumkapı, which have grown savvy to the tourist hordes that trample through, that of Samatya–a thoroughly authentic neighborhood by the southwestern edge of Istanbul's city walls–seems to be frequented mostly by Samatyans.

The feeling upon entering this small plaza of meyhanes and fish stands is that you've wandered into the kitchen of a very hospitable, curious family. The atmosphere is small-town main street à la Turca, where a text message from America is a newsworthy event.

We had headed to Samatya to check out this homey village vibe and explore its small streets dotted with Greek and Ar-

34

menian churches, but we stayed because of the hamsi and cold beer on offer at Küçük Ev, a corner fish shack with but a few tables.

The Black Sea anchovies were plump and finger-length, their silver streak capturing our attention like a fishing lure saying, "eat me." The grill man took a handful and dusted them with red pepper flakes and thyme before tossing them on a flat-top grill, flipping them quickly

and then plating them. The hamsi were so moist and tender that they seemed to liquefy on the tongue.

The accompanying salad was most notable for its dressing of lemon, olive oil and tangy pomegranate molasses, which perfectly balanced the bittersweet range of rocket greens, carrots, dill, red onions, scallions and carrots. With very reasonable prices, this is one of the best deals in town. ◆

Meşhur Unkapanı İMÇ Pilavcısı

Atatürk Bulvarı, Unkapanı
(Near the "İMÇ Çarşışı 1. Blok"
sign on the east side of the
street, on the way to the
aqueduct. Look for the crowd.)

THE (RICE) FREAKS COME OUT AT NIGHT

There are probably hundreds of pilaf carts crisscrossing Istanbul every day, but one on Atatürk Bulvarı, a busy road in Fatih, is different. While the owners of other carts usually roll along trolling for business, this one stays put each night, letting the crowds come to him. And they do. Every night, a large group of men can be seen huddled around the brightly lit food cart, stuffing their faces in a kind of zombie-like frenzy. The cart serves up a pilaf of rice, chickpeas and chicken along with ayran (a salty yogurt drink)–comfort food that comes at a very comforting price.

"We've been in the same spot for 15 years," said the cart's operator, a man in a starched white chef's smock who would only give his first name, Ayvaz, for fear of getting in trouble with the authorities. "We're famous– that's why there's always a crowd here," he said, while furiously dishing out servings of pilaf on small metal plates.

Ayvaz certainly knows what he's doing: the buttery rice in his pilaf was deeply flavorful, tasting like it was cooked in chicken stock.

The perfectly cooked chickpeas, meanwhile, added texture to the pilaf, which was topped with thin chunks of moist chicken breast. For a final touch, most of the people around us added a squirt of ketchup, something that we also tried, and approve of.

The ayran, poured from a small wooden cask resting on top of the rice cart, was the perfect drink to wash down the pilaf.

The crowds that gather every night around Ayvaz's cart may be the best testament to the power of his pilaf. But there's another–imitators. Following in Ayvaz's footsteps, other cart operators have started to set up shop along Atatürk Bulvarı, offering the same basic pilaf and ayran combo. But Ayvaz doesn't seem to be worried. "Those guys aren't pilaf makers," he said. "They're pirates." ◆

Şehzade Erzurum Cağ Kebabı

GAUCHO KEBAB RIDES AGAIN

Istanbul has plenty of kebab joints, but places serving cağ are sadly hard to find. Cağ Kebabı, which originated in the eastern Anatolian province of Erzurum, looks like a horizontal döner but tastes otherworldly. As we see it, cağ is the Turkish equivalent of Argentina's asado or the Brazilian churrasco–a kebab for serious meat lovers. Fortunately, we've found an excellent place to keep getting our cağ fix: Şehzade Erzurum Cağ Kebabı, not far from the Sirkeci train station on pedestrian-only Hocapaşa Sokak.

The restaurant has only a handful of tables, all within whiffing distance of the spit, where cuts of expertly marinated lamb slowly cook over a wood fire. As the horizontal spit slowly turns, the meat continuously bastes itself, occasionally flaring up with a sizzle and a pop that chars an outlying corner of meat. Unlike with döner, where the dönerci saws and hacks from his vertical spit, leaving the meat he has cut off lying in a puddle of grease, the cağ man carefully selects each morsel of meat from the spit with a sharp knife and a small, thin skewer. A dönerci's work has more in common with that of a lumberjack, but doing cağ right requires the patient and steady hands of a skilled surgeon. When he's done he'll present you the skewer, threaded with a precious collection of tender yet crispy bites, served on top of a toasty warm piece of lavaş.

Şehzade offers more than just cağ. We also recommend the hearty red lentil soup to start the meal and a small plate of piquant Ezme (a salad of finely chopped tomatoes, onions and parsley) to go along with the meat. The restaurant even serves a very tasty dessert: the state-fair-worthy Kadayıf Dolma, a fat torpedo made out of shredded wheat wrapped around a core of chopped nuts and then deep-fried and doused with a sticky sweet syrup. ◆

Sürt Şeref Büryan Kebap Salonu

THE LAMB UNDERGROUND

Kadınlar Pazarı, a pleasant, pedestrian-only square in Istanbul's Fatih neighborhood, is the closest the city has to a "Little Kurdistan." Small markets and butcher shops selling honey, cheeses, spices and other goodies from Turkey's predominantly Kurdish southeast region surround the square.

There are also numerous restaurants, most selling Büryan Kebap and Perde Pilav, two dishes that are specialties of Siirt, a city that's home to both Kurds and Arabs. Büryan is a bit like Turkey's version of

Texas pit BBQ. A side of a small lamb is slowly cooked over coals in a deep hole in the ground, resulting in exceptionally tender meat covered in a thin layer of fat that has turned crackling crunchy.

For perde (meaning "curtain" in Turkish), a fragrant and peppery pilaf made of rice, chicken, almonds and currants is wrapped in a thin pastry shell and then baked inside a cup-shaped mold until the exterior turns golden and flaky. When done right, both dishes are the kind of food that leaves you thinking about it fondly for

İtfaiye Caddesi 4,
Fatih
212 635 8085
9:30am-midnight

days–even weeks–after you've eaten it. Siirt Şeref Büryan Kebap Salonu is a büryan and perde joint that leaves us begging for more.

Originally from Siirt, the restaurant's proprietors claim to have been in the büryan business since 1892. "Cooking in the pit makes the lamb tastier," says owner Levent Avcı. "You don't need any spices or anything else to make büryan taste good." The restaurant's Büryan Kebap is served with

the meat cut into small cubes and placed on a round flatbread (which soaks up the fat), sprinkled with a touch of salt.

As for the Perde Pilav, its flaky pastry shell is not so thick that it overwhelms the rice and chicken mixture inside, but not so thin that it doesn't have any crunch. When you cut through the pilaf's shell, a cloud of aromatic steam rises upwards. ◆

Vefa Bozacısı

STRANGE BREW

After our first taste, we were not quite ready to sing the praises of boza, a thick drink made from fermented millet. But, as it did to us, the drink may haunt you, much like the call of the itinerant boza vendors who wander the streets of Istanbul during the winter months calling out a long, mournful "booooo-zahhh."

It's a taste all its own, bearing the sour mark of the fermented grain and the sweetness of the sugar added during the fermentation process.

The consistency is that of a milkshake that can't decide if it wants to be thick or thin, while the texture is all Gerber's. Boza is served in a glass with a spoon, a layer of sprinkled cinnamon and roasted chickpeas floating on the top. The first few spoons are beguiling, the palate fooled by the cinnamon and utterly sidetracked by the crunchy chickpeas. The contrast of the cinnamon makes the boza seem sour at first, but soon after, a subtle sweetness

emerges in the chilled unadulterated boza below. Perhaps better than the taste of the drink is the experience of ordering and consuming it at Vefa Bozacısı, a tavern-like boza outlet where this Ottoman culinary tradition has been protected with a flourish since 1876, when the current owner's great-grandfather first opened shop.

The place remains carefully preserved, down to the worn marble doorstep and antique wooden bar. We like to sit in the corner below the case holding a glass from which Atatürk, the founder of the Turkish Republic, enjoyed a glass of this strange brew (the alcohol content is about 1%), just as sultans must have before him. In short, an order of boza at Vefa is indeed a cultural experience.

And like other obligatory cultural experiences, say the opera or a visit to a science and industry museum, you are allowed to sigh with relief when your glass of boza has finished. ◆

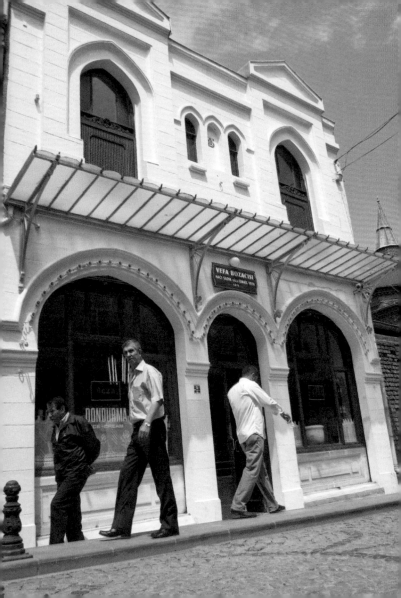

Türk Dünyası Kültür Evleri 6,
Kültür Parkı, Topkapı
212 567 1077
10:30am-10:30pm

Zinnet Restaurant

SILK ROAD TRIP

The hearty food of Central Asia is surprisingly hard to find in Istanbul, despite Turkey's proximity and strong ethnic bonds to the region. So we were glad to find Zinnet, an appealing Central Asian restaurant located deep inside a recently created "Kültür Parkı" just outside the old city walls. Zinnet is inside the park's Turkic republic complex, home to a gaily decorated yurt and several small wooden buildings that act as mini showcases for the Turkic republics of Central Asia.

Run by a Uighur family from the city of Urumqi in western China, the restaurant has an airy, slightly upscale feel to it. The extensive menu is a kind of Silk Road culinary greatest hits collection. A small complimentary salad arrived, made of thin slivers of a crunchy vegetable we couldn't recognize—uncooked potato, it turned out! Bathed in a red pepper and sesame oil dressing, the salad packed a flavorful and satisfying punch.

A soup called Çüçüre, made of a spicy broth with delicious little tortellini-like meat-filled dumplings floating in it, hit the spot.

Zinnet's Uighur-style mantı, gyoza-sized steamed dumplings filled with roughly chopped fatty meat and topped with zingy malt vinegar and spicy pepper oil, were outstanding. The fragrant Zireli Kebap, a stir-fry of beef and onions, had the look of a Chinese dish but the earthy spicing of a Middle Eastern one.

We ended our meal with an order of Lagman, the handmade noodle dish that's a Central Asian staple. Although good, the noodles lacked the depth of character of those we've tasted elsewhere.

Considering the rustic style of the food, Zinnet might seem a bit pricey. Then again, since the only other way to taste what Zinnet serves would be to book a flight to Tashkent or Kashgar, the place is a bargain—with a great location, to boot. ◆

Note: To get to Zinnet, take the Zeytinburnu-Kabataş tramway and get off at the Topkapı station, just outside the city walls (not near Topkapı Palace).

The Grand Bazaar:
Come for the Shopping, Stay for the Food

Photos: Melanie Einzig

We like to think of Istanbul's Grand Bazaar–open since 1461–as the world's oldest shopping mall. If that's the case, shouldn't the Grand Bazaar be home to the world's oldest food court? That may be taking the analogy too far, but for us, the Grand Bazaar can be as much a food destination as a shopping one. As we see it, one of the hidden pleasures of going to the bazaar (once you get past the overzealous shopkeepers hawking souvenirs) is exploring some of its quieter back alleys and interior courtyards for new dining possibilities, especially some of the smaller restaurants that cater not to tourists but rather to the locals who work in the sprawling marketplace. **These places are some of our favorites:**

GAZİANTEP BURÇ OCAKBAŞI

A friend directed us to this small Grand Bazaar eatery and we are now forever in her debt. Located on a narrow side street off one of the bazaar's busier thoroughfares, this unassuming grill house serves up very tasty Gaziantep-style food. (Gaziantep, a city in Turkey's southeast, is considered one of the country's culinary capitals.) Our Ali Nazik, tender morsels of marinated beef sitting on a bed of a garlicky yogurt-eggplant puree, was perfectly made. The delicious salad served on the side, topped with chopped walnuts and zingy pomegranate molasses, was impeccably fresh. We were even more excited about the restaurant's specialty: extremely flavorful dolmas, made out of the shells of dried eggplants and red peppers that are rehydrated and then stuffed with a rice and herb mixture and served with yogurt on the side.

Gaziantep Burç Ocakbaşı only has a few tables, which are lined up along the length of the alleyway that is the restaurant's home. The ambiance is provided by the strings of dried egg-plant and peppers that hang above the tables, the smoke and sizzle coming from the grill and the thrum of bazaar activity all around.

**Parçacılar Sokak 12,
Grand Bazaar
212 527 1516
noon-5pm; closed Sunday**

HAVUZLU

Figuring out what to eat is easy here. A large steam table at the front of the restaurant's open kitchen holds a daily assortment of some 25 dishes, including a variety of meat and vegetable stews that we like to think of as Turkish soul food–homey, well-made and fresh. After you make your selection, waiters in black vests and matching ties swiftly bring the food to your table in the slightly tacky 500-year-old dining hall, which has large Ottoman-style blown glass chandeliers hanging from its vaulted ceilings.

Gani Çelebi Sokak 3,
Grand Bazaar
212 527 3346
11am-5pm; closed Sunday

In a certain way, Havuzlu, which is named after the small havuz (fountain) in front of the restaurant, makes us think of what a Denny's restaurant might have looked like in Ottoman times: a well-oiled machine serving up comfort food for weary travelers. Of course, rather than burgers, grilled cheese sandwiches and Grand Slam breakfasts, Havuzlu serves spinach stew with yogurt, döner, creamed eggplant and, for dessert, stewed figs with kaymak (Turkish clotted cream). The only proper sit-down place in the Grand Bazaar, Havuzlu may no longer be a secret, but its location, in a quiet corner of the market, gives it the feeling of a refuge–a place to hide out once the shopping has worn you down.

KARA MEHMET KEBAP SALONU

This is one of our favorite places, not only in the Grand Bazaar but in all of Istanbul. The restaurant, a tiny hole-in-the-wall, serves the usual assortment of kebabs–including, for the daring, kidney and liver kebabs–all expertly grilled by the mustachioed usta (or "master"). A testament to the appeal of Kara Mehmet's kebabs: we went there with a vegetarian friend who was so taken with the restaurant's Adana Kebap that he ended up taking his first bite of meat in 30 years.

Food aside, what really draws us to Kara Mehmet is its location, deep inside the open-air courtyard of the Cebeci Han, one of the Grand Bazaar's numerous out-of-the-way caravanserais. Compared to the bustle in the rest of the bazaar, Cebeci Han is an oasis of peace and calm, mostly filled with small shops where people repair rugs, rather than sell them. Even the owner of the one actual rug shop inside the courtyard seems more interested in playing backgammon with his friends than moving carpets. When you're done with your kebab, order Kara Mehmet's delicious Künefe for dessert and a tea from the small teahouse next door and enjoy the behind-the-scenes look at bazaar life.

İç Cebeci Han 92,
Grand Bazaar
212 527 0533
11am-5pm; closed Sunday

Upper Beyoğlu

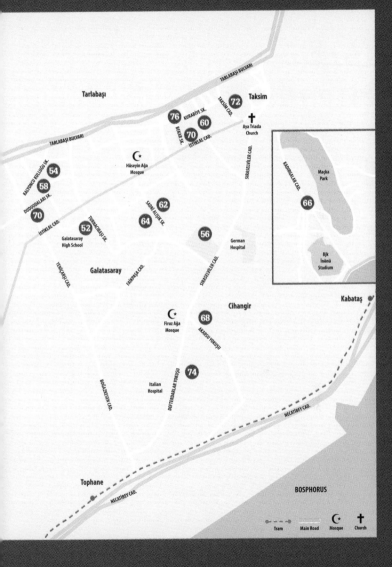

Kartal Sokak 1/A,
Beyoğlu
212 244 5575
noon-1am; closed Sunday

Çukur Meyhanesi

WHEN LIVER MET HAMSİ

It wasn't quite as dramatic as Meg Ryan's big moment at Katz's Deli in "When Harry Met Sally," but a guttural moan of pleasure was detected from our table when we tasted the shredded celery root in yogurt, a house specialty meze at Çukur Meyhanesi. And we weren't faking it. We eat more meze than we care to report and, while most are fine, few can be considered orgasmic.

Çukur Meyhanesi, a small, slightly shabby basement meyhane, doesn't look like the kind of place with shining stars on the menu. But that's a grave misunderstanding: at Çukur, it's all about the food. That garlicky yogurt loaded with celery root and purslane, topped with a barely detectable drizzle of olive oil and flax seeds, is enough to ensure a return visit. The charred red peppers with crushed walnuts, evoking both spicy and smoky tones, was also a winner. And two meyhane staples–Patlıcan Salatası, a smoky puree of eggplant, and Soslu Patlıcan, cubes of fried eggplant in a tangy tomato sauce–were expertly made and reminded us why they are such classics. Then there was the ciğer, or liver. Sliced into thin strips that are lightly fried and then dusted with red pepper, this ciğer was exceptionally smooth in texture and mellow in flavor; if we're not mistaken, it brought out another moan of pleasure at our table.

Unusually, the folks at Çukur have also figured out how to grill Black Sea anchovies, or hamsi. Long considered a lost cause by grill men for their tendency to slip through the grill, hamsi are usually fried or baked. At Çukur they work about ten of the squirmy little fish onto a skewer, bookending them with tomato and pepper. Hamsi is agreeable in just about any form, but fresh off the grill the fish's characteristic taste is even more pronounced. Side by side, hamsi and ciğer are a perfect pairing: a poor man's surf and turf. ◆

Dürümzade

WRAP ARTISTS

Istanbul's after-midnight dining choices tend to be of the offal variety–tripe soup, chopped lamb's intestines–thought to be curatives after a night of hard drinking. Luckily, there are other options. Dürümzade, positioned right on the fringe of the rowdy, bar-lined streets of Beyoğlu's fish market, makes a dürüm, or Turkish wrap, that's equally satisfying at 2am or 2pm.

If a sandwich is only as good as its bread, then any dürüm discussion is all about the lavaş, the Turkish flatbread used to make it. Dürümzade's thin, ovular lavaş, rubbed with a mix of red pepper and spices, is far from the stiff, uniform discs found at many other dürüm joints. Like a good thin pizza crust, it's filled with textural variations, bubbles, crispy edges and moist chewy pockets. Stacked and hidden away, it incubates in a drawer below the charcoal grill.

The choices of fillings are Tavuk Şiş (chicken kebab), Adana Kebap (spicy minced beef) or Urfa Kebap (mild minced beef). The skewered meat is put on a grill, which is fanned to the desired heat by the portly fellow guarding the lavaş. After one

Upper Beyoğlu

Kamer Hatun Caddesi 26/A
Beyoğlu
212 249 0147
open 24 hours

rotation of the skewer, the grill master pulls out a wrap and drapes it over the kebabs cooking over the coals, creating a smoky tent for the meat while keeping the lavaş off of the fire directly. As the lavaş tent heats up, the spice rub on the wrap imparts its flavor onto the skewered meat below.

While the lavaş is still flexible, the usta (or "master") pulls it from the grill and covers it with a bed of chopped parsley, sumac-dusted onions and tomatoes, onto which he lays the freshly grilled meat from the skewer. Then, like a cowboy deftly rolling a cigarette, he rolls the dürüm. Before handing it over to the now salivating customer, he puts the whole thing back on the grill for a final crisping. Now that's a wrap. ◆

Hayvore
Lost and Found

The name of this restaurant, in the Laz language of the Black Sea area, means, "I am here." In the case of Hayvore, the "I" refers to shaggy-haired owner Hizir, who has struck out on his own after making his mark at another Beyoglu Black Sea restaurant, Sisore ("Where are you?" in Laz). With the help of some of Sisore's kitchen staff, Hizir has been able to create some of his own Black Sea magic at his new restaurant.

The Black Sea area is Turkey's culinary misfit; it's not really about kebabs or meze. If anything, the food there seems to have been mysteriously transplanted from the American Deep South. We're talking corn bread, collard greens and smoky bean stews. It's simple, filling, down-home food, and Hayvore is a great—and afford-able—spot to get acquainted with it. It serves some of the best Black Sea food we've had in Istanbul.

We highly recommend the hamsi (fresh anchovy) pilaf, the holy grail of Black Sea cooking. A kind of savory fish cake, the very tasty pilaf has small hamsi filets wrapped around a thick bed of rice infused with herbs, currants and pine nuts.

Everything else we've tried at Hayvore has been a winner. A rib-sticking stew made with kale, beans and hominy was earthy and smoky. If this weren't Muslim Turkey, we'd swear someone had slipped a ham hock into the pot. Hayvore also serves up a fine version of another Black Sea staple: creamy white beans (kuru fasulye) cooked up in a rich, buttery red sauce.

On any given day, Hayvore will have more than a dozen items bubbling away on the steam table—some typical Black Sea dishes, some not. It's the easiest way to visit the Black Sea without leaving Is-tanbul ◆

56

Muammer Usta,
Kamer Hatun Cad. 13/A,
Beyoğlu
9am–6pm

Şinasi Usta,
Sahne Sokak 18, Balıkpazarı,
Beyoğlu
212 245 4312
9am–6pm

Kelle Söğüş vs. Kelle Tandır

FACE/OFF

Here we tackle one of the great barroom debates of these parts: is a sheep's head, or kelle, more tasty when boiled and served chilled or roasted and served hot?

Based on looks alone, Muammer Usta's Kelle Söğüş–head boiled and served cold–was decidedly the underdog. A bit gaunt and ashen, this skull looked a bit past its prime. But watch this Cinderella story unfold. Muammer Usta went to work with a sharp knife, transforming the sheep's skull into a beautiful plate of thinly sliced meat dusted with salt, onions and parsley.

Şinasi Usta's Kelle Tandır, roasted golden brown and steaming from its thick meaty brow, looked like a born champ. Şinasi Usta whacked it to pieces with a cleaver, carefully removing the brain, cheeks, tongue and countless bits of juicy joint meat, which he shredded with his fingers for the drooling judges. The brains had a nutty richness and the consistency of peanut butter,

while the cheeks and the thin strip along the jaw reminded us of the best bite of a roasted lamb–tender, juicy meat with a crackle of skin. The firm, lean tongue was otherworldly. However, the bite of fat from the back of the eye (which is the source of a well-known Turkish declaration of endearment) left something to be desired.

Muammer's Kelle Söğüş fought a different fight. Whereas Şinasi Usta's meat was juicy and soft with fat, Muammer's was lean and firm. If Şinasi's kelle looked like a nice mess of BBQ, Muammer's more resembled a carefully planned plate of cold cuts with clean and crisp flavor.

As both had great merit, deciding a winner would prove difficult. But then, out of nowhere, a knockout punch came in the form of a plate of heavenly pure cheek meat delivered, gratis, by another customer who claimed to have eaten söğüş once a week since 1962. And the winner is: Muammer's Kelle Söğüş. ◆

Muammer Usta's Kelle
Söğüş (boiled and
served chilled)

Şinasi Usta's Kelle
Tandır (roasted and
served hot)

Kurabiye Sokak 7,
Beyoğlu
212 243 7637
11:30am-5pm

Köfteci Hüseyin

THE CADILLAC OF MEATBALLS

Köfte may seem like nothing more than grilled meatballs to non-locals, but, like New Yorkers with their pizza, Turks take köfte very seriously. We like to get our fix from Köfteci Hüseyin, a humble purveyor in Beyoğlu who got his start selling meatballs from a pushcart grill some 40 years ago.

Although at one point the cart was traded in for a tiny storefront just off Taksim Square, Köfteci Hüseyin still keeps it very real, with some of the best meatballs in town. On the wall is a picture of the founder from the days when he had little more than a pair of tongs and his grill. Though Hüseyin has since passed on, he bequeathed his tongs to his son, who now works the grill and maintains a winning recipe that combines quality, consistency and low prices. While some places lard their köfte with breadcrumbs, giving them a somewhat rubbery consistency, Hüseyin's patties distinguish themselves from the rest with an unusually high meat content. The silver-dollar-sized patties are also quite plump, allowing them to remain juicy inside while their exterior gets pleasantly charred on the grill.

Enter this humble shoebox of an eatery and before you can grab a seat you'll be asked, "One portion or one and a half?" Shortly thereafter: "Side of beans?" An order of Piyaz, a salad of white beans and onion, is to köfte what coleslaw is to BBQ. Dressed in olive oil and vinegar and served chilled, this classic side is a köfte house mainstay that shouldn't be missed. That's about all there is to ordering in a traditional Turkish köfte joint—and tradition is what Köfteci Hüseyin is all about.

As you eat your portion and a half of Hüseyin's köfte, served along with a big hunk of fresh bread, a dollop of spicy red pepper sauce and fresh chopped onions, you'll understand why these are not "just meatballs." ◆

Sadri Alışık Sokak 11,
Beyoğlu
212 249 5208
6:30am-11pm

Lades 2

A BEYOĞLU GREASY SPOON

The no-frills Lades 2 presents diners with that age-old question: what to eat first, the chicken or the egg? A Turkish version of the American-style greasy spoon diner, Lades 2 specializes in all things fowl, from chicken soup to a variety of egg dishes and even a dessert that (we kid you not) weds a thick, milky pudding with chicken.

Lades 2 is located on a side street off İstiklal Caddesi, in a lively area filled with cafes and small nightclubs specializing in Turkish folk music. It's just across the street from the original Lades but has a more proletarian vibe, with tables of mostly unaccompanied men scarfing down their food in a kind of monastic silence, broken only by the waiters shouting to the short-order cooks in the back.

The menu is basic. If it's chicken you want, order the restorative soup– not far off from what you would get in a Jewish deli in New York–which comes with little strands of noodle floating in it. Or try Tavuk Yağda, a stir-fry of shredded chicken and hot green peppers in a tangy tomato sauce. Eggs come two ways: fried or scrambled with sautéed onions, green peppers and tomato in a dish called Menemen. Most patrons order their fried eggs cooked together with either sucuk (a garlicky Turkish sausage), pastırma (dried cured beef) or even ground beef. It's greasy goodness, served up in its own individual skillet.

Of course, no visit to Lades 2 would be complete without a taste of their excellent Tavuk Göğsü (literally, "chicken breast") pudding. You won't be biting into chunks of bird in your pudding. Rather, the meat is poached and then pounded until it is nothing but wispy fibers, adding texture and the subtlest flavoring to the white pudding, which is served with a dusting of cinnamon. Don't be scared to order it. After all, you know what they do to chickens at Lades 2. ◆

Lades

OLD FAITHFUL

If Lades, which means "wishbone" in Turkish, provided an actual wishbone alongside the usual post-meal wet wipe and toothpick, we'd close our eyes and make a wish that we could eat their Tandır Kebap, or oven-roasted baby lamb, seven days a week. These large knots of tender, fragrant meat lined with a soft cushion of fat are the sort of high-calorie lunch that we might save for a special occasion, but Lades regulars take for granted.

Lades is an old-school spot, a classic local lokanta serving stews and steam table favorites day in, day out. The monogrammed flatware, faded from decades of use by diners sopping up that last bit of stew with a fresh piece of white bread, indicates the sort of customer approval that we seek in a lunch spot. On one visit, we tried the hotpocket-like Talaş Kebap, a stew of beef, carrots, currants, onions and pine nuts wrapped in phyllo dough. With a bowl of lentil soup, a side of okra

and, for dessert, Kazandibi ("burnt pudding"), we discovered that just about everything at Lades is highly soppable and dependably good. Indeed, if Lades were an automobile, it might be an old Volvo station wagon–nothing exotic, but safe and extremely reliable. "Most of our customers are regulars. They know exactly what is served on which day of the week. How could we possibly change anything?" said manager İlker Bey.

As it is written (on the window out front), on Mondays and Thursdays you shall eat Döner Kebap in succulent ribbons served over rice. Tuesday is a day for Arnavut Ciğeri, lightly fried lamb's liver ramped up with red peppers. Smothered okra, spinach with rice, roast chicken, various stews and our beloved Tandır Kebap are available every day but Sunday, when the restaurant is closed. They may be dependable, but even the guys at Lades deserve a day of rest. ◆

Mehmet Ercik's Sucuk Sandwich Stand

TOP DOG

Just as London's Savile Row is known for its tailors, and New York's Canal Street for its cheap handbags, Istanbul's Kadırgalar Caddesi is surely known to all as sucuk central. On any given evening, in this street running between the hills of Maçka Park and the nearby Açıkhava open-air theater, the sidewalks are alive with itinerant sausage stands.

Sucuk is a dried sausage eaten throughout the region surrounding Turkey, with slight variations on the same theme of ground beef, spiked with salt, red pepper

and other spices. Prior to hitting the grill, it is not the most appetizing sight, usually found hanging from hooks in supermarkets and butcher shops in uniform crimson links that look like a beaded curtain of very fat hot dogs.

But once it's relieved of its paper-like casing, chopped into bite-size chunks and put on the grill, you understand what all of the fuss is about. The charcoal fire quickly revives the sausage from its sheathed slumber into sizzling disks that let off an aroma trail that can bring traffic to a standstill, as it does

on Kadırgalar Caddesi. Mehmet Ercik has been slinging sucuk on these streets for more than a decade, first from a minivan and, more recently, from a street stand. He serves the sucuk on a half loaf of white bread or lavaş.

We prefer the latter with grilled peppers, onions and an additional blast of red pepper paste (just say "acılı olsun").

Though perhaps not the most sophisticated sausage-eating experience, a sucuk sandwich is satisfying in the same way that a Chicago hot dog "with everything on it" can be: the whole is definitely greater than the sum of its parts. Except in very cold or bad weather, Ercik sets up his stand along Kadırgalar Caddesi around 9pm and keeps grilling into the early morning hours, depending on demand. ◆

Özkonak

THE REAL PUDDING SHOP

Regulars at Özkonak, a well-loved fixture in Cihangir's ever-changing restaurant scene, must cluck in disapproval at the sight of a new generation of customers who walk right past the pudding display at the front and head for the steam table and its selection of prepared savory dishes in back. Though the lunch specials here are quite tasty, Özkonak is a pudding shop at heart and should be approached accordingly. To fill up on stuffed eggplant and beans before dessert is to deny yourself the sweet milky pleasures that have made this a neighborhood institution for almost 50 years.

Tavuk Göğsü, chicken breast pudding, is most often mentioned in travelers' tales alongside salted Oaxacan iguana and deep-fried Vietnamese cobra. But unlike so many other bizarre edibles, the pudding doesn't taste like chicken at all. The chicken is merely a texturing agent in this thick, milky pudding roll, bringing an unexpected–though pleasant–fibrous feel to what you'd expect to be smooth. However, we prefer Tavuk Göğsü's poultry-less cousin, Kazandibi ("bottom of the cauldron" in Turkish), whose caramelized bottom layer gives it firmness and a smoky-sweet finish. We also often opt for Keşkül, an almond-based custard colored Day-Glo yellow. Just watching the seemingly radioactive pudding arrive at the table is exciting. Dusted with crushed almonds, Keşkül and a tea is a perfect mid-afternoon snack.

If you still have room for a main course after a couple of rounds of dessert, make your way to the back and you'll find the steam table, stocked with well-made standards. Stuffed cabbage, stewed vegetables, baked meatballs with fingerling potatoes and pilaf are usually on offer. But if you don't make it to the mains, no one will fault you. After all, this is a pudding shop. ◆

Dudu Odaları Sokak 3,
Balık Pazarı, Beyoğlu
212 249 2469
6am-10pm

Sakarya Tatlıcısı

JUST DESSERT

Autumn is quince season in Turkey and that means the appearance of one of our favorite desserts, Ayva Tatlısı ("quince dessert" in Turkish). The apple-like quince is one of those complicated, mysterious fruits that take on a new life when cooked. Raw, quinces are often astringent and inedible. Cooked–with a generous amount of sugar–the fruit assumes a different personality and a new-found depth of flavor.

To make Ayva Tatlısı, large quinces are halved, stewed and baked until they turn meltingly soft and are coated in a thick, sticky reddish glaze; the color is the result of a chemical reaction that is yet another of the fruit's mysteries.

Once cool, the quince is served with a dollop of kaymak, the heavenly Turkish clotted cream. The addition of kaymak, whose buttery richness cuts through yet deliciously compliments the sweetness of the glazed fruit, takes the

dessert to almost sinfully good levels (think of it as a refined jelly donut). Ayva Tatlısı can be addictive, and Sakarya Tatlıcısı, located within Beyoğlu's fish market, is a perfect spot to get a fix. In business for more than 50 years, the small pastry and sweets shop has a certain old-world charm. In the fall, its display case always holds a tray of the glistening quinces next to its usual assortment of baklava and other traditional sweets.

While many other places spike their Ayva with food coloring, turning it radioactive red, at Sakarya the fruit is left to its own devices, achieving an ethereal color that hovers somewhere between rosy pink, ruby red and burnt orange. Although most people get their quinces to go, we like to sit at one of Sakarya's two tables, order a tea and take in the atmosphere of the fish market.

We would go there more often, but sadly (or, perhaps, fortunately), quinces are only available a few months of the year. ◆

Şimşek Pide

IT'S BETTER WITH BUTTER

Turkey's take on the pizza comes in two distinct varieties. There's the round, Arabesque lahmacun, and then there's pide, a more substantial canoe-shaped creation that's a specialty of Turkey's Black Sea region. In Istanbul, pide joints are almost as common as blaring car horns, but Şimşek Pide Salonu has won our loyalty for its consistently outstanding made-to-order pide and convenient location on a quiet, sunny side street just off of Taksim Square.

To simplify the ordering process, Şimşek's menu features a pide pictograph. The pide comes in three general forms: round like a pizza, the more traditional oblong open-faced pide, or the calzone-like Kapalı Pide. The main components remain the same, regardless of the shape: dough plus toppings, assembled and then fired in a pizza oven. At this particular venue we prefer the open pide with a few toppings. The usta, or "master," rolls the

dough out long and thin and pinches up a ridge along the edges, forming the crust, which will bubble up and crackle around a chewier center, much like a good Italian pizza pie.

Then comes a generous helping of Black Sea kaşar, a rich but mild cow's cheese that hints at mozzarella. Depending on your preferences, he adds tomatoes, peppers, pastırma (slices of cured beef) or ground beef. If you so desire, he'll even crack an egg over your pide before sliding it into the oven on a long wooden paddle.

A few minutes later the pide emerges with a nicely browned crust and soft, moist center. The final touch is a thorough glazing with melted butter. The Black Sea region is known for its top-tier dairy products. However, we suggest a pat of butter, rather than a dousing. Just tell the chef, "az tereyağı."

That said, we would agree with the usta at the oven, who explains, "It's just not pide without butter." ◆

Defterdar Yokuşu 52/A,
Cihangir
212 293 6437
7am-7pm

Van Kahvaltı Evi

THE BREAKFAST CLUB

In Turkey's predominantly Kurdish eastern provinces, breakfast is not just for breakfast anymore. Particularly in Van, the morning repast has been turned into serious business: the town is filled with kahvaltı salonları ("breakfast salons") serving a dizzying assortment of farm-fresh breakfast items day and night.

In recent years this boffo breakfast has worked its way westward, and several Van-style "breakfast salons" are now open in Istanbul. Van Kahvaltı Evi (Van Breakfast House) in Cihangir has quickly become one of the area's most popular, and it's easy to see why. The people running the friendly place–a crew of hip youngsters who seem to be members of the slow food movement without even realizing it–serve a mean Van breakfast, bringing in most of their ingredients, some of them organic, from back East.

The Van breakfast takes the traditional Turkish breakfast of cheese, tomato, cucumber and bread and turns it up several notches.

At Van Kahvaltı Evi, along with the standards, your breakfast plate comes with an assortment of Van cheeses (including a very tasty one that contains brined wild herbs), the heavenly kaymak, tangy Cacık (thick yogurt spread) and Murtuğa, a heavy wheat flour porridge. Butter, jams, olives and some of Van's famous honey round all this out, along with endless glasses of strong tea. One plate is enough to feed a whole family.

The restaurant also serves fried eggs and Menemen, scrambled eggs cooked with sautéed onions, green peppers and tomato. The Gözleme, thin sheets of hand-rolled dough wrapped around cheese, potato or spinach, is also excellent.

Van Kahvaltı Evi can get quite busy on the weekends, so come early if you want to get a table.

Or, better and easier yet, do like they do in Van and come later in the day to have breakfast for dinner. ◆

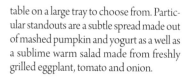

Zübeyir Ocakbaşı

THE MEAT IS ON

Finding a kebab restaurant in Istanbul is not hard; there must be thousands. But finding the right kind of place can be surprisingly difficult. Some of the no-frills kebab joints are very good, but they don't make for a night out. On the other hand, some of nicer places–where you can find a more extensive menu and drink booze with your dinner–take things too far. (Tuxedoed waiters serving kebabs? Griller, please!)

This is what makes Zübeyir Ocakbaşı, a fantastic grill house in Beyoğlu that always seems to be packed with large groups having a very good time, such a refreshing find. They serve seriously good food without taking themselves too seriously. Occupying two cozy floors in a historic building near İstiklal Caddesi, the restaurant is dominated by a long hearth topped by a copper hood, where the meat is grilled over hardwood coals.

Meals at Zübeyir usually begin with a round of mezes, brought to your table on a large tray to choose from. Particular standouts are a subtle spread made out of mashed pumpkin and yogurt as well as a sublime warm salad made from freshly grilled eggplant, tomato and onion.

The Gavur Dağı salad, a mix of greens, herbs and tomatoes in a piquant pomegranate molasses dressing, is also good.

From there, it's on to the kebabs. The standard grill items are all outstanding. The Adana Kebap (spicy minced lamb) has just the right combination of meat, fat and red pepper. Kanat (chicken wings) and Pirzola (lamb chops) are also superbly grilled.

Zübeyir also serves up some cuts of meat not found at most kebab joints, such as the tasty Tarak (lamb spare ribs) and, for the more adventurous, Koç Yumurtası, or ram's testicles (which, we must admit, we have yet to try).

It's not easy to stand out in a city filled with kebab restaurants, but Zübeyir does it effortlessly. ◆

Street Food

We're especially fond of Istanbul's vibrant—and sometimes plain wacky—street food scene. Here we present a highly subjective look at our favorite street foods and some of the best places to get them.

The plaza in front of the Galata Tower, Galata
no phone

THE GALATA CUCUMBER MAN

We've never learned his name, and he goes into hibernation every winter. But we eagerly await the reappearance in the spring of the vendor we know simply as the "cucumber man of Galata," a chubby fellow with Coke bottle glasses who sells what may be the city's simplest, yet most satisfying street food: peeled and salted cucumbers, a fresh green rebuke to all those starchy and fried snacks out there.

Beginning in late spring, when the weather starts to warm up, the cucumber man parks his rickety little cart in the plaza in front of the Galata Tower, where he stays until the weather turns in the fall. His method is simple: take a chilled cucumber, peel it, slice it twice down the middle so that it splays out like a flower, and salt it generously.

It may sound basic, but on a hot summer's day, the cucumber man usually has a good crowd that gathers around his cart clamoring for this refreshing bite. (He recently branched out and started selling carrots and apples, too.) At less than a lira a cucumber, it's a snack that's hard to refuse.

KIZILKAYALAR'S WET BURGER

The sign may read "Wet Burger" ("Islak Burger" in Turkish), but there's a lot more to say about Kızılkayalar's moist mini patties than that. How about "Heavenly Slider," "Binge Drinker's Delight," or "The Best 2 Lira Ever Spent in Taksim Square?"

The Kızılkayalar experience starts from a distance, usually late at night. It begins with a whiff of garlic detected well across Taksim Square; then, through the bustling crowd, eyes lock onto the bright lights of the steam box holding the burger bounty. Hungry customers are finally tugged in, like a tanker on the Bosphorus, by the steady foghorn voice of the Kızılkayalar hamburger man bellowing, "Buyurun, buyurun!" (Roughly: "Come and get it!")

Make no mistake, the burger is wet, having been doused by an oily, tomato-based sauce before incubating in a glass-lined burger hamam. There, it becomes even wetter, the once fluffy white bun rendered a greasy, finger-licking radioactive shade of orange, both chewy and slick on either side of the garlicky beef patty. Like an order of nachos at the movies, the wet burger is a sinful pleasure that flies in the face of our otherwise high culinary standards. But at 2am on a Friday night, nothing is as good as a Kızılkayalar wet burger–except for another one.

**Sıraselviler Caddesi 6,
Taksim Square
no phone
open 24 hours**

Mumhane Caddesi 83-85,
Karaköy
212 244 7775
6am-7pm; closed Sunday

ÇITIR BAKERY'S SİMİT

Let's hear it for the (deceptively simple) simit. With only a few ingredients to its name, this sesame-encrusted bread ring has become the most ubiquitous snack in Istanbul, the undisputed heavyweight champ of the street food scene. In fact, in recent years, the plucky simit has gone to even greater heights: once only sold from carts and by itinerant vendors carrying wooden trays on their heads, the snack is now the headlining act at several new, nationwide fast-food chains.

But despite its crisp exterior and tough street cred, the simit is actually a softie. Like a delicate flower that begins to wilt as soon as it is plucked out of the ground, the simit starts to fade as soon as it leaves the oven. By the time many simits reach the streets, they are already past their prime and heading towards making better hockey pucks or paperweights than snacks.

That's why we prefer to get our simit straight from the source. One of our favorite bakeries is Çıtır in the Karaköy neighborhood, where the gruff Emir Özdemir has been manning the oven for 20 years. All day long, he turns out tray after tray of hot simit. Fresh out of the oven, the simit reveals its complexity, the contrast between its crispy-crunchy exterior and its soft, steamy interior more defined, and the earthy, nutlike flavor of the almost charred sesame seeds that coat it more pronounced. The knockout punch? All of this for less than one lira.

SABIRTAŞI'S İÇLİ KÖFTE

For years, in one calm spot on İstiklal Caddesi, just beyond Galatasaray High School, stood the beatific Ali Bey, an angel in a white doctor's coat offering salvation in the form of golden fried İçli Köfte. Though he passed away recently, Ali Bey left his post and his street-side stand–as much a part of the İstiklal streetscape as the red trolley cars and belle époque apartment buildings–to his son, who fills it with the same panache, white jacket and all. And thanks to Ali Bey's wife, Fatma Hanım, the İçli Köfte lives on.

Known as kibbeh in the Arab world, İçli Köfte is a savory snack consisting of a bulgur wheat shell that holds a filling of ground meat, onions, parsley and spices. These little torpedoes are handmade upstairs by Fatma Hanım, who spends most of the day at a large table with her daughter-in-law working the stuffing into the casing before passing them on for final preparation. They chat and laugh as they work, their hands working by what appears to be instinct alone–a scene more reminiscent of a rural family kitchen than a dining room with a view of one of Istanbul's best-known streets.

Though the İçli Köfte are also served boiled, in the Sabırtaşı restaurant five flights up from the street-side stand, we prefer the ones served on the street: fried to perfection, crunchy but not too greasy on the outside, and moist on the inside. Unlike many of Istanbul's İçli Köfte, which often look and taste like a fried mini football, Sabırtaşı's are a refined delicacy. It's as if each grain of bulgur and every bit of filling were specifically designed to rise into a spicy, steamy, heavenly waltz across the palette as the fortunate snacker breaks the crunchy seal of the outer crust. Sabırtaşı's İçli Köfte gets our vote for the number one street food in Istanbul.

İstiklal Caddesi 112,
Beyoğlu
212 251 9423
noon–midnight

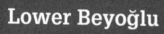

Lower Beyoğlu

Minare Sokak 21/A, Asmalımescit
212 292 1100
noon-midnight; closed Saturday
lunch, and Sunday

Antiochia

STYLE AND TASTE

In Istanbul, we've noted an inverse relationship between a restaurant's atmosphere and what's coming out of the kitchen. But just when we thought this theory was watertight, we stumbled upon Antiochia, a small restaurant that exudes cool without sacrificing flavor. From its funky logo to the hipster waiters, Antiochia clearly has a different ambition (and clientele) than most restaurants serving food from Turkey's southern Hatay region. A meal at your own pace here is a relaxing experience and the kitchen keeps it very real in the Hatay tradition.

Nar Ekşili Cevizli Közbiber, a divine relish of red and green peppers in pomegranate dressing, was topped with crushed walnuts, adding a crunchy texture to this sweet and sour cold starter. Tasting the homemade yogurt with mint proved just how little we knew about what yogurt can be: pleasantly sour, pungent and almost as thick as butter. Muam-

mara, a thick spread of walnuts, red pepper, spices and pomegranate extract, is a Hatay signature and a fine choice, but our favorite is the Kekik Salatası, an intense meze of green olives, fresh thyme and olive oil. We recommend ordering the mixed meze plate, served with a basket of crisp lavaş chips, which allows you to sample all seven meze and save room for the main course.

Antiochia's main courses are simple, recognizable dishes, set to a higher frequency. Şiş Et is a plate of marinated cubes of beef skewered and grilled over a charcoal fire. On any given evening in Beyoğlu, there must be thousands of skewers of Şiş Et coming off the grill, but none are quite as tender and succulent as at Antiochia.

The minced meat dürüm (wrap) with onions and tomatoes, an Istanbul street food favorite, is among the best we've had in the city. Finally, a place where style doesn't come at the expense of what's being served. ◆

Beyoğlu Öğretmenevi

THE TEACHER'S LOUNGE

Like Atatürk statues and crescent-and-star flags, the öğretmenevi ("teacher's house") is an integral part of the Turkish landscape. Found in almost every city in Turkey, these government-run institutions serve as affordable guesthouses for educators and those traveling on a teacher's budget. They are for the most part drab affairs, but not so in Istanbul's historic Beyoğlu neighborhood, where the local öğretmenevi is a grand old building dating back to the late 1800's, formerly a French-built hotel that put up some of the same Orient Express travelers who stayed at the more famous Pera Palace Hotel nearby.

An öğretmenevi since the 1980's, the building received a complete remodeling a couple of years ago, resulting in the addition of a top-floor restaurant and bar. The modernish dining room has several tables with fine views of the waters of the Golden Horn and a cozy, five-stool bar at one end. Reserva-

tions are a must on most nights, especially if you want one of the few tables with a view.

The menu holds no surprises–the usual mezes and kebabs, along with grilled fish–but the prices are unheard of for this swanky part of town, especially for a place with a view. The lamb chops we ordered were not exceptional, but, like the meze, no worse than anything you get in any of the meyhanes along Beyoğlu's touristy Nevizade Street. "Mexican Steak," a filet of beef covered in a tomato-mushroom sauce and melted cheese, seemed like a high-concept take on school cafeteria food, but was surprisingly good. More than the food, what will keep us coming back to the öğretmenevi is the unpretentious bar and its wonderful view, especially in summer, when the restaurant's big windows open up. It may not be the finest dining experience in Beyoğlu, but it's certainly one of the more memorable. ◆

Çukurcuma Köftecisi

A MOM AND POP MEATBALL SHOP

Having lunch at Çukurcuma Köftecisi is like being a part of the live studio audience of a TV sitcom–with meatballs.

Plotline: Three generations of an unusually tall family run a busy local restaurant with what seems like very little service industry experience but great intentions and strong will. Hilarity ensues.

Characters: Mom is the kitchen talent, deserving of the poofy chef's toque she sports. Dad is the enforcer in the tank top and apron, known to flare up like the charcoal fire he tends.

The two sons are more interested in roaming around the neighborhood on the delivery scooter than waiting tables. And Grandpa in the fedora, from his post at the door, just wants to know who took his last cigarette. Add a cast of quirky regulars and you've got a picture of lunch here.

But there's nothing funny about the food at this down-home neighborhood eatery. There's

always a soup cooked from scratch, sautéed vegetables and a hearty stew. Mom's Revani, a semolina cake soaked in a sugary syrup, is so light and delicate it nearly crumbles at the nudge of a fork. If you want lamb chops or köfte, you'll have to speak with Dad. The köfte are charred and meaty and served with a small salad, Turkish pilaf and french fries.

Saturday is fry-day and the first batch is ready just around noon. Mom's Kadınbudu Köfte, battered and fried patties made out of ground meat and rice, are excellent, but the Mücver, zucchini fritters, are truly outstanding.

When plating these unusually fluffy, almost omelet-like beauties, Dad carefully pats each one with a spoon of garlicky yogurt and drizzles a bit of tomato sauce over that. Lunch at Çukurcuma Köftecisi, in the heart of Beyoğlu's antiques district, is a perfect midday show: good cast, good food, and a punch line that everyone gets–a great lunch for not much money. ◆

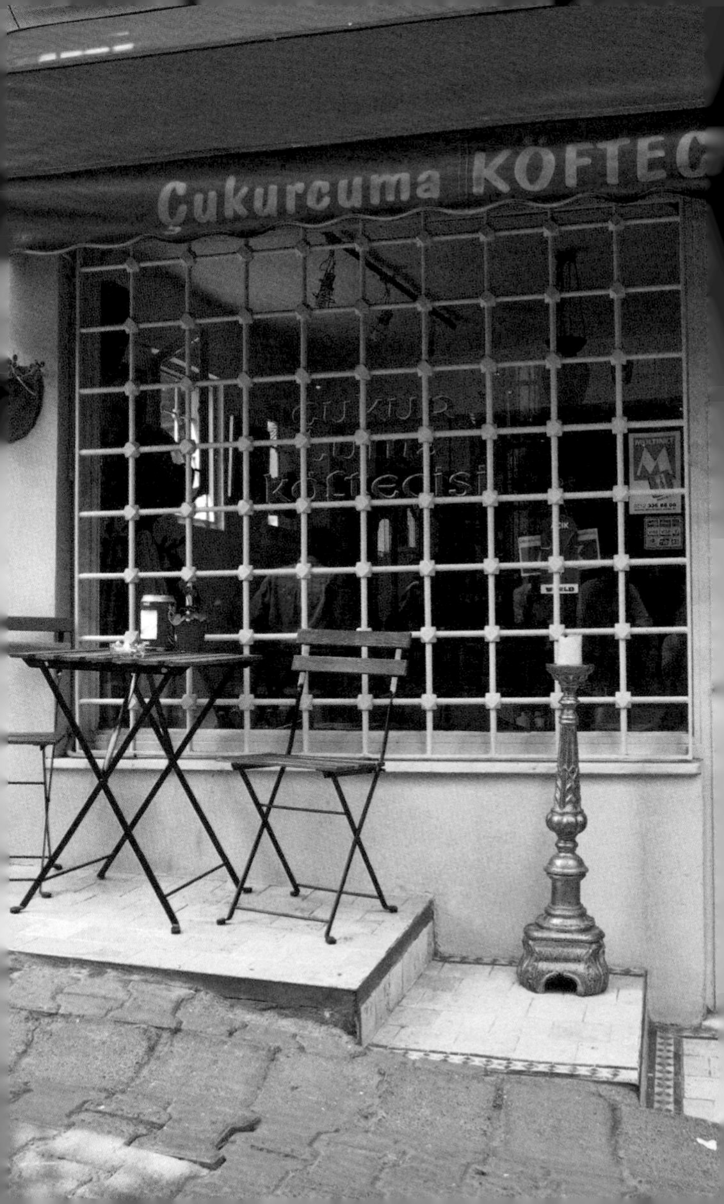
Çukurcuma KÖFTEC
köftecisi

Fıccın

THE CAUCASIAN SENSATION

According to our Turkish-English dictionary, the word "Çerkez" means "Circassian," but in our book it is synonymous with "delicious." As evidence, look no further than Fıccın, a friendly restaurant serving the unique cuisine of the mountains of the Caucasus. Many Turks trace their roots to this culinary Xanadu, including the folks at Fıccın, who have put together a Turco-Circassian menu that includes specialties from both kitchens.

Cold chicken and walnut spread (Çerkez Tavuğu), found on many Turkish menus, is here a bit richer and redolent with red pepper and garlic. Tulen, an aromatic chicken soup, is an unusual surprise in a country so loyal to the lentil. Shreds of chicken lace the thick slow-cooked stock, whose garlicky essence travels with the steam nose-ward, a whiff of ecstasy.

The Çerkez take on the dumpling is similar to a pierogi, filled with meat or potatoes and served in a bath of yogurt and light red pepper oil. Though the menu describes the restaurant's namesake dish, Fıccın, as Circassian börek, this is not the flaky pastry sold throughout Turkey. In this case, savory, almost cake-like dough is layered over fragrant ground meat and then baked like a pizza. One slice of Fıccın is best shared among the table.

Unfortunately, the Çerkez dishes on the menu stop here. On the other hand, Fıccın's Turkish standards–though found on the menus of numerous other restaurants–are particularly well-made. Notable among them is the sublime Karnıyarık, baked eggplant stuffed with peppers, onions, minced meat and tomatoes.

Though open for dinner, Fıccın thrives on its bustling lunch scene, when its three dining rooms and clusters of outdoor tables fill quickly. Turnover is quick, so be sure to come early or you might miss the daily specials. ◆

İsmail Kebapçısı

LAHMACUN TYCOON

Where Beyoğlu slopes down towards the Bosphorus in rough-around-the-edges Tophane, there's not much in the way of swanky eating. The dietary staple of the neighborhood is a spicy flatbread called lahmacun. At İsmail Kebapçısı, owner İsmail smiles broadly from his post by a blackened stone oven. İsmail grills up mincemeat and chicken kebabs, but he clearly takes the most pleasure in plucking a small handful of dough, dusting it with flour and rolling it out matzo-thin on the marble slab before him. He pats on top of it a fine spread of ground meat, tomato, onion, red pepper paste and spices and then shoves it deep into the hearth with a long paddle.

There have got to be a dozen other lahmacun makers within a four-block radius of İsmail. "Why is his lahmacun different?" you may ask. "Because I think positively!" İsmail explained one day, eyes twinkling. We're not inclined to doubt him on that point. Positive thinking goes a long way in the kitchen and the proof is right there on the end of his paddle. And İsmail is not the only one who thinks positively about his lahmacun.

The commercial strip that's home to his restaurant is teaming with esnaflar, or the offices of small tradesmen, who can be famously finicky about what they eat and how much they pay for it.

At lunchtime, İsmail turns out steaming lahmacun as fast as he can for a delivery boy who sprints off to waiting customers. Though it might resemble a wafer-thin, cheese-less pizza when it emerges from the oven, think of lahmacun as a kind of wrap. Before being rolled up, the lahmacun is loaded with a mound of fresh cut parsley and an optional squeeze of lemon.

A bite of this is at once spicy and tart, hot and cold, smoky and fresh, crispy and chewy. Such simple contrasts add up to a very complex snack. One of Istanbul's best street eats–positively! ◆

Kebapçı Enver Usta

UNDERGROUND FAVORITE

Kebapçı Enver Usta, a subterranean kebab joint, hits the spot when we're looking for a simple and satisfying lunch. Finding Enver Usta is part of the fun. Located for the last 20 years on a quiet Beyoğlu alley that thankfully has been bypassed by the neighborhood's gentrifying wave, the restaurant occupies the bottom floor of what seems like an abandoned building, the only sign of life a lone flowerpot on one of the window ledges.

Things get livelier once you step down the stairs from the sidewalk and into the restaurant. On most days, Enver Usta is packed to the gills with locals who are either eating at one of the few tables or waiting for one to open up. At the far end of the restaurant stands Enver Usta himself, a skinny and slightly hunched-over man with a serious gaze and an occasionally surly manner. While he tends to the smoky grill, Enver also barks out orders at the tireless Ahmet, the joint's sole waiter for the last 14 years.

Enver Usta carries the standard array of kebabs and does them all just right. We're partial to his tasty Adana Kebap, made of minced meat mixed with red pepper flakes.

We also enjoy the chicken kebab and wings, both marinated in a piquant red pepper sauce, and the Çöp Şiş, tiny cubes of tender beef grilled on a skewer.

When you order, be sure to ask Ahmet for a plate of the excellent Ezme Salatası, a salad made of finely chopped red onion, tomato, red pepper and parsley, and of the equally good bulgur pilaf, as well as a plate of lavaş, thin flatbread that's great for wrapping around the kebabs. At the end of your meal, get an order of the excellent baklava that's delivered to the restaurant daily.

We tend to leave Enver Usta feeling stuffed. That's when we encounter the real danger of eating in an underground restaurant—getting up the pitched stairs on a very full stomach. ◆

Olivia Geçidi 1/A, Beyoğlu (Near the St. Antoine Cathedral on İstiklal. Look for Barcelona Patisserie on the corner.)

Mandabatmaz

GROUNDS FOR CELEBRATION

It's a dirty secret nobody wants to talk about: finding a good cup of Turkish coffee in Turkey can sometimes be very difficult. This is no small matter, since Turkey, after all, is the land that helped introduce coffee to the rest of Europe during Ottoman times. One person who clearly understands this is Cemil Pilik, brewmaster for the last 17 years at Mandabatmaz, a tiny café that makes one of Istanbul's finest cups of Turkish coffee. The stuff Pilik serves lives up to what Turkish coffee should be—and it better, since the café's name roughly translates as "so thick even a water buffalo wouldn't sink in it."

Pilik's excellent brew is thick to the point of being almost chocolaty, each demitasse holding only a few sips' worth of strong coffee before you hit a rich deposit of dark brown grounds. "Not everybody can do this," Pilik says, as he holds a well-worn copper coffee pot to a blue gas flame that shoots out like a jet from a small, two-burner range. "It's all in the hand," he adds, making a twisting motion with his wrist. Also important is the coffee. Mandabatmaz's comes freshly roasted and ground every day, arriving in unmarked, clear plastic bags. "It's roasted just for us; it's not commercially packaged," Pilik says, opening up a bag of coffee to let us sniff its aroma.

Along with Turkish coffee, Mandabatmaz also serves freshly made tea (which gets very good reviews).

The café itself, located on a quiet alleyway off İstiklal Caddesi, is barely large enough to hold Pilik, the marble counter he works behind and a giant, silver samovar that dispenses hot water for the coffee and tea. Most customers end up sitting outside, on one of the dozens of small stools that line the alleyway, some chatting happily with friends, others silently drinking Pilik's coffee, as if it were a kind of elixir. ◆

Corner of İstiklal Caddesi and
Deva Çıkmazı
(across from the Salad Station)
6:30am-11am

Mehmet Demir's Breakfast Cart

THE WHEEL DEAL

Mehmet Demir may not be one of Istanbul's better-known restaurateurs, but he is certainly among its shrewdest. He runs a bustling business that has customers literally lining up in the street to taste what he serves, which is a monstrous and delicious breakfast sandwich. Demir is part of Istanbul's great food on wheels tradition, with carts that sell everything from rolls to grilled meatballs making appearances throughout the city at different times of the day and even according to the seasons. Although Demir works from a cart, there's something more permanent about his operation. For the last 11 years, he and his wife Ser have been selling their sandwiches from the same corner of pedestrian-only İstiklal Caddesi every morning from 6:30am until about 11am or until they run out of bread, whichever comes first.

The three-wheeled wooden cart is topped with a glass - lined box that holds crusty, bakery-fresh mini loafs on the top shelf, and below that, a smorgasbord of breakfast ingredients: feta and string cheese, sliced tomatoes, green peppers, parsley, hard-boiled eggs and some mystery meat he calls "chicken ham." Most of Demir's customers–hungry office workers on their way to their jobs–get all of the above crammed into a loaf that first gets treated with a schmear of zesty black olive paste. (We prefer to order ours "etsiz," without the meat.)

The way all the ingredients work together, from the salty tang of the cheese and olive paste to the crunch of the pepper, the coolness of the tomatoes to the freshness of the parsley and the pleasing unctuousness of the egg, makes for something very satisfying. More discerning types, meanwhile, order the "bal-kaymak" sandwich, a loaf spread with honey and the dreamy Turkish version of clotted cream.

A very fine way to start the day. ◆

Eski Çiçekçi Sokak 3,
Beyoğlu
212 252 6052
noon-1am

Mekan

THE COSMOPOLITAN

Sometimes billed as "that Armenian-Jewish restaurant in Beyoğlu," Mekan harkens back to the neighborhood's cosmopolitan past, when it was home to a large non-Muslim population. The food is sometimes Sephardic and Armenian, sometimes Turkish, but the important thing is that Mekan is a good restaurant that turns out authentic traditional favorites.

For our mezes, we sampled the pickled mezgit (English whiting); an ultra-fresh tomato salad with crushed walnuts, dressed with pomegranate molasses; and a plate of smoked red peppers in a thick, sour yogurt. We also tried the Topik, an Armenian specialty made out of chickpeas, potatoes, tahini and onions that are mashed together and turned into a mound that is then studded with pine nuts and dusted with cinnamon.

This sweet and savory concoction is a novelty that people either hate or write folk songs about, but should be tried at least once.

Among the hot appetizers, we suggest the İçli Köfte (known as kibbeh in Arab countries), which is ramped up with a bit more spicy heat than usual. Its deep crimson color alone speaks of the paprika kick within.

Patlıcan Börek is a Mekan specialty from the Sephardic kitchen that is also not to be missed. In place of cheese, spinach or potato, this börek's crispy phyllo dough shell holds a smoky eggplant mash.

Entrées at Mekan tend towards simple arrangements, mostly from the grill. Köfte (meatballs) or a fresh fish are always around. When they're on offer, we opt for a plate of hamsi (Black Sea anchovies) in cornmeal cooked on a griddle, a preparation that does this small fish justice.

Mekan's uncommon ethnic specialties, served in a quiet atmosphere, present a nice change of pace from the predictable menus and raucous surroundings of most of Beyoğlu's meyhanes, and keep us coming back for more. ◆

Orhan Adlı Apaydın Sokak 11/A,
Beyoğlu
212 244 2543
11am-4:30pm; closed Sunday

Şahin Lokantası

EDIBLE COMPLEX

For Turks, mealtime is often a complicated emotional drama, one that revolves around a lifelong effort to return to the culinary womb—in other words, their mother's kitchen. Mom's cooking sets the standard by which all others are judged. Of course, it's difficult to sneak home in the middle of the busy workday for a taste of Mom's cooking—which is where the esnaf lokantası comes in. Although roughly translated as a "tradesmen's restaurant," it's really an extension of the home kitchen, a place where the spirit of everyone's mother seems to be stirring the pots.

Open since 1967, Şahin Lokantası is an esnaf lokantası that very successfully manages to put the "home" back into home cooking. The restaurant is usually bursting at the seams during lunch, with an almost comical number of people stuffing themselves into the small, two-story space, and you will likely eat your meal at a table full of strangers.

The menu changes daily, with about a dozen dishes usually on offer, a combination of meat or vegetable stews, pilafs, köfte (meatballs) and assorted other classics of the Turkish (home) kitchen.

We've found nothing but winners at Şahin's. The İmambayıldı, made out of a fried eggplant stuffed with onions, tomatoes and garlic, is among the finest renditions of this totemic dish that we've had in Istanbul. "Albanian" liver, small cubes of tender and un-"livery" meat that have been dusted with flour and red pepper flakes and then fried, is also outstanding. Şahin's superb Sütlaç (rice pudding) reminds us of what's missing in so many of the other Sütlaç around town: rice.

Şahin's version is chockablock with grains of soft rice floating inside a thick, milky pudding. It's delicious, comforting, and—like everything else served in the restaurant—just like what "Mom" makes. ◆

Sofyalı 9

KEEPING IT REAL IN ASMALIMESCİT

It's hard not to feel pangs of nostalgia when walking through Beyoğlu's booming Asmalımescit neighborhood these days (and nights). It may be hard to believe when you see it today, but only a few years ago most of Asmalımescit was dark at night, lit up only by a few dive bars, small restaurants run by eclectic chefs and old-time meyhanes, among them Sofyalı 9. Back then, Sofyalı seemed slightly out of place in the neighborhood, its menu, décor and service several notches above its local competition. These days, fortunately, the restaurant still seems out of step with what's happening around it, serving up a healthy dose of old-school Asmalımescit charm that none of its chichi new neighbors have.

We like to think of Sofyalı not as a meyhane but rather as a Turkish bistro. Don't come here if you want to end your night with a rakı-fueled dance on the tables to the ac-companiment of a gypsy band. This is a place to depend on: the menu has all the meyhane classics, from meze to fish, and rarely changes; the food is always good; and the service always friendly. It's a place that works on any night, be it a romantic dinner for two on the warmly lit ground floor with its big windows looking out onto the street, or a festive meal for ten on one of the restaurant's upper floors, which have a cheerful Greek taverna-like vibe. Sofyalı 9 is also a great spot for lunch, with a limited menu of homey specials that changes daily.

In good weather, we recommend making a reservation for one of Sofyalı's highly coveted outdoor tables. They make a great perch from which to take in Asmalımescit's newly bustling street life while at the same time soaking up a good dose of what made the area great to begin with. ◆

Turkey exists in a kind of alternative culinary universe where liver, or ciğer, is not the punch line of a joke or the basis of a bad taste memory that haunts you for life, but rather something that's sought out. In parts of eastern Turkey, ciğer's popularity often trumps that of other cuts of meat. Edirne, a city near Turkey's border with Bulgaria and Greece, is so famous for the dish that some Istanbulites make day trips there just to eat fried liver. After several years in Turkey, we've even found ourselves under liver's powerful spell, our previous disdain for the organ now gone.

At two of our favorite liver joints in Istanbul, the formula for the dish is almost the same. Tiny cubes of tender lamb's liver are grilled over hardwood coals on long, thin skewers. The kebab is still unmistakably liver, but its taste and texture are much more delicate and simply less "liverish" than what'd expect. (You can ask the waiter for a "yarım porsiyon," or half portion, just to give it a try.) The real fun is in what comes along with

Liver, My Dear?

the liver. Before the skewers even arrive, your low table is piled high with plates of parsley, mint, arugula and slightly charred grilled onions and peppers dusted with red pepper. With these comes a serving of Ezme, a mix of extremely finely diced tomatoes, onion and parsley flavored with tart pomegranate molasses that is made by a knife-wielding usta, or "master," who lords over a well-worn cutting board near the grill.

The skewers arrive along with a pile of very thin wraps, which are used to grab the meat off the hot skewers and are then filled with a bit of everything that's on the table, rolled up and eaten in two or three flavor-filled bites. If you order a dürüm, the chef will do all the work and make a giant wrap for you stuffed with grilled meat, fresh herbs and onions.

Here are our two favorite liver restaurants in Beyoğlu:

CANIM CİĞERİM

Canım Ciğerim, a fun and tasty kebab spot in Beyoğlu's Asmalımescit area, makes things easy. The menu only has two items from which to choose: the restaurant's namesake dish ("canım ciğerim" is actually a Turkish expression that translates into "my liver, my dear," used as a term of affection), or what is simply referred to as "meat." Fortunately, for those not interested in taking the liver plunge, Canım Ciğerim's "meat" (or et, in Turkish) option is an extremely fine one. In this case, small morsels of tender beef are skewered and grilled and served with the same condiments that come along with the liver. Whether liver or "meat," we've found that having a bad meal at this lively restaurant is not an option.

Minare Sokak 1, Beyoğlu
212 252 6060
weekdays noon-midnight,
weekends noon to 3am

CİĞERİMİN KÖŞESİ

As longtime fans of Canım Ciğerim, we of course noticed the arrival of Ciğerimin Köşesi (roughly translated as "my liver's corner"), a gleaming new kebab spot with a somewhat similar-sounding name and even some of Canım Ciğerim's former waitstaff working there. Though we initially ignored what we believed to be an upstart copycat, it turns out this new addition to the liver scene just might give the original a run for its money.

Ciğerimin Köşesi offers the usual choice of tasty liver or beef kebabs and the condiments that come with them, but unlike its rival, it also serves up superb chicken kebabs, the skewers threaded with very moist chunks of white meat that have been marinated in a red pepper sauce. Although we tend to order beef kebabs, Ciğerimin Köşesi's chicken kebabs have us reconsidering our preferences.

Tütüncü Çıkmazı 3/A,
Beyoğlu
212 245 7777
9am-midnight

Galata and the Docks

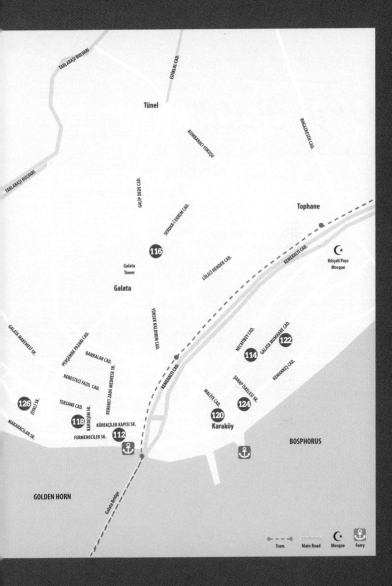

Fermeneciler Caddesi Ali Yazıcı
Sokak Gümrük Han 10, Karaköy
212 244 9776
11am-3am

(Restaurant is located behind
the fish market in Perşembe
Pazarı. There are several
outdoor fish places in the area,
so be sure to confirm that you
are sitting at Akın.)

Akın Balık
(THE OTHER) KARAKÖY FISH HOUSE

Just around the corner from Karaköy's fish market is Akın Balık, a barebones, inexpensive fish restaurant. Just a few steps from the Golden Horn, the place has a laid-back vibe that makes us feel like we're no longer in the big city but instead relaxing in some seaside village. We like to head over for an early dinner as the sun sets over the water, a time of day when Karaköy seems to sigh and relax for the evening.

Akın, a gray-mulleted, leather-vested fellow, seems to help set that mood, with his slow gait, slight smile and soft touch with customers. He runs his place with nothing more than one grill and a cooler, so service can be a little slow. Luckily the cooler is stocked with cold cans of beer, which are served discreetly wrapped in brown paper, ostensibly to "keep the heat away."

Unlike most of the other simple fish joints around here, which exclusively sling sandwiches or Hamsi fry-ups, Akın serves a tasty fish soup every day, a hearty, almost chowder-like fish stock amped up by bright carrot slivers and chopped parsley. Akın is also a reliable place to try some of those street foods that we are not quite comfortable buying from Istanbul's roving, teenage shellfish dealers, like fried mussels or mussels stuffed with rice. But be forewarned, they often run out before nightfall.

Whole grilled fish, be it levrek (sea bass), çipura (sea bream), or sarıkanat (small bluefish), is about as fresh as it gets. But we suggest an old Istanbul street food favorite that used to be sold from boats on the Golden Horn: the fish sandwich. A grilled bonito filet nestled in a hollowed-out half loaf of bread, dressed with onions, parsley and lettuce, is a simple pleasure that goes perfectly with sitting on a stool in the setting sun while drinking Efes beer from a can wrapped in brown paper. ◆

Mumhane Caddesi 35/B,
Karaköy
212 244 0347
8:30am-8:30pm

Beşaltı Kirvem

TURKISH FOR "TAQUERIA"?

One of the downsides to Istanbul's otherwise great food scene is the lack of a credible Mexican option. But when our craving for Mexican gets strong, we don't despair; we just head to Beşaltı Kirvem Tantuni, a hole-in-the-wall (literally) spot whose food and atmosphere remind us of the tiny taquerias in Mexico and the U.S. that we so miss.

Tantuni is one of Turkey's classic–though shamefully lesser-known–street foods. For the dish, thin strips of beef are grilled, somewhat like Mexican carne asada, and kept warm on the side of a massive circular pan with a concave depression in the middle. When an order is made, the cook scoops up some of the beef and reheats it in the middle of the pan in a steamy combination of oil and water, creating a thin gravy. In the meantime, he warms up a long piece of lavaş, a flatbread that's the Turkish equivalent of the tortilla, on the side of the pan, let-ting the lavaş soak up some of the meat's juices. Once the beef is warmed up, he piles it on top of the lavaş–along with tomatoes, sumac-dusted onions, parsley and a combination of spices, including cumin and red pepper–and rolls it up into a long, thin torpedo that can be gobbled down in a few quick bites. Served with only a side of hot peppers, it's simple but delicious.

Tantuni originated in Mersin, a city on Turkey's Mediterranean coast best known for, well, being the birthplace of tantuni. From there, the dish has gone on to become a street food staple in other parts of Turkey. In Istanbul, the backstreets of Beyoğlu have loads of tantuni shacks that do bustling business, particularly late at night. But we've found Beşaltı Kirvem, which caters to a lunchtime crowd in the more commercial Karaköy neighborhood, to be in a league of its own. It's a two-for-one deal: the best tantuni and–we like to pretend–Mexican in town. ◆

Serdar-i Ekrem Sokak 2,
Beyoğlu (Kuledibi)
212 252 4853
11am–midnight

Fürreyya

THE BEST LITTLE FISH HOUSE IN GALATA

From the outside, Fürreyya Galata Balıkçısı, a tiny restaurant in Beyoğlu's quaint Galata area, doesn't look like much. But inside this modest fish shack beats the heart of a more ambitious venue. The friendly husband and wife team who own the place and share kitchen duties used to run a restaurant in Istanbul's upscale Bebek neighborhood, and it's clear that Fürreyya is in experienced hands.

Located on a busy corner only a stone's throw from the 13th-century Galata Tower, the restaurant offers a great (and affordable) alternative to eating at one of Istanbul's fancier fish restaurants, where often you pay too much buck for the bang.

Fürreyya's menu is basic, the bulk of it devoted to whole fish either grilled over hardwood coals or fried in a light dusting of flour. The exceptionally fresh fish, a selection of whatever is in season in the waters around Istanbul and other parts of Turkey, is found in a small refrigerated display case outside the restaurant.

The menu also holds some very rewarding surprises. Balık Köftesi are delicious fish cakes cooked over the charcoal grill and served with a squeeze of homemade basil aioli. On occasion, Fürreyya serves up its tasty take on mantı, tortellini-like miniature pockets of dough that are usually filled with ground meat but here are made with fish. The highlight of the menu, though, may be its most humble offering: the Balık Dürüm, a tortilla-like wrap filled with grilled fish and caramelized onions. It's one of Istanbul's best and tastiest deals.

If the tiny restaurant is full, Fürreyya's owners will happily take your order and wrap it up to go. From there you can take your food and eat it in the pleasant square that lies in the shadow of the nearby Galata Tower, where you can sit down on a bench and enjoy your lucky catch. ◆

Tersane Caddesi,
Kardeşim Sokak 45, Karaköy
212 243 4080
7pm-midnight

Grifin

SEAFOOD OASIS

In the charmingly ramshackle back-streets of Karaköy's Perşembe Pazarı, the dining scene is decidedly no-frills. Which makes Grifin–a high-end seafood restaurant where cocktails are served on a rooftop terrace with sweeping views–a baffling culinary mirage. Grifin is, in fact, the nocturnal alter ego of Tarihi Karaköy Balıkçısı (TKB, from here on), a lunch spot long considered one of the best addresses in town for a no-nonsense, pure fish dining experience. Located on the top floor of the same building as TKB, it shares a kitchen, menu and waitstaff.

We started with a bowl of fish soup–more a chowder than bisque–teeming with tasty chunks of fish, diced potatoes, carrot slivers, bay leaves and lemon.

Among the hot appetizers was a unique tempura-like dish made with fresh anchovies, the batter crisp, light and slightly sweet. We also approved of the calamari, whose gar-licky yogurt sauce tasted just fine on a piece of bread once the squid ran out.

There is no showmanship on the fish side of the menu, no special sauces or pyrotechnics. Extremely high standards of quality and freshness, meanwhile, keep the daily fish offerings limited. Fortunately, the menu has two TKB favorites. Kağıtta Levrek, sea bass cooked in paper, arrived steaming in its paper vessel, the boneless flesh succulent and tender, with a fragrance of tomatoes, peppers and lemon wafting out at us. We were equally pleased with the Dil Şiş, plump little fillets of sole that are rolled up and grilled on a skewer and that brought to mind a sea scallop with their sweet flesh and creamy texture.

Grifin seems to be positioning itself to compete with the fancy fish houses up the Bosphorus, and it has TKB's reputation to back it up. But for now at least, it still feels like an unpretentious local spot, albeit one with white tablecloths. ◆

Rıhtım Caddesi Katlı Otopark
Altı 3-4 (main store) or
Mumhane Caddesi 171
(factory store), Karaköy
212 293 0910 (main store) or
212 249 9680 (factory store)
7am-10pm

Güllüoğlu

STILL FLAKY AFTER ALL THESE YEARS

Karaköy Güllüoğlu is one of our favorite places in Istanbul for the pure baklava experience. Located a stone's throw from the Bosphorus, this baklava emporium has been catering to Istanbul sweet tooths since 1949. Done up in borderline tacky décor that looks like it's meant to evoke late Ottoman splendor, the place serves more than a dozen kinds of phyllo-based sweets, none of them resembling the cardboard-like baklava that is often dished out outside the Middle East.

Aside from its excellent classic baklava, made with either pistachios or walnuts, we are also fans of Güllüoğlu's Şöbiyet, a gooey, triangular-shaped phyllo pastry filled with pistachios and cream, and of a specialty called Sütlü Nuriye, made of flaky layers of pastry drenched in a sweet, milky sauce. After picking out what you want from the display cases holding large trays of baklava, you can either eat your sweets standing up at one of several high tables inside, surrounded by an unmistakably buttery aroma, or sit down at a table outside and catch the Bosphorus breeze.

Like most baklava makers in Turkey, Güllüoğlu's founders hail from Gaziantep. (There are actually dozens of families from there with the same name manufacturing baklava throughout Turkey, which can make things confusing.) Although they have ramped up their production over the years, the place still seems to be sticking with tradition. Güllüoğlu has also stayed true to its Karaköy roots, still making its baklava in the neighborhood, at a facility just a few minutes' walk from its main store. You can eat baklava there too, gaining perhaps a few minutes of freshness over what's found at the main location, though the atmosphere is decidedly less fancy. Both spots open bright and early at 7am– in time to catch the morning rush of baklava addicts. ◆

Mumhane Caddesi 24,
Karaköy
212 249 1772
noon-4pm; closed weekends

İstiridye Balık Lokantası

THE BUSINESS OF LUNCH

Mumhane Caddesi, in the waterfront Karaköy area, has so many good restaurants along it that it acts as a kind of culinary vortex, radiating a magnetic pull that we find hard to resist. One day the street's siren call brought us to İstiridye Balık Lokantası, an old-fashioned fish restaurant that caters to a lunchtime crowd of local office workers and executives. The people who come to İstiridye expect the restaurant to serve food whose quality doesn't vary because, it would appear, many of them seem to come here every day.

İstiridye had intrigued us over the years; we had always walked by but never gone in. The entrance, in dark wood and exuding something of a private club aura, seemed less like a doorway and more like a portal into another time and era. Yet the prices listed on the dry-erase board at the front were firmly 21st century. Inside, serious-faced waiters in crimson vests and crisp ties hustled about from table to table.

The menu was basic. A delicious chowder-like fish soup, green salad and a small assortment of fresh fish, most of them–perhaps so that the busy clientele don't have to work too hard to eat their lunch–deboned, skewered with green pepper and onion, and grilled over coals.

We chose the Dil Şiş, thin strips of flounder rolled up and grilled on a skewer. The fish was superb, the outside slightly charred and crisp, the inside moist and tender. The table next to us ordered Levrek Şiş, large chunks of sea bass fillets that were also skewered and grilled, which also looked very tasty.

We finished our meal off with a simple glass of tea, delivered from a nearby teahouse by a worker who dutifully stood at the entrance to İstridye and waited for one of the waiters to take the tray from him, as if he knew that crossing that t h r e s h o l d meant something more than simply entering a restaurant. ◆

122

Kemankeş Caddesi 37,
Karaköy
212 292 4455
6am–midnight

Karaköy Lokantası

A DOCKSIDE WINNER

Tucked into the street behind the yet-to-be gentrified docks at Karaköy, among shops advertising boat tickets to Odessa and cubby-sized import and export offices, is the neighborhood's culinary port of call, Karaköy Lokantası. With great food, personable service and tasteful décor, this family-operated eatery defiantly proves that a good dining experience doesn't have to come with a shocker of a bill.

Karaköy Lokantası is best known as a power lunch spot, with Hünkar Beğendi, a leftover from the Ottoman imperial kitchen, the midday star of the menu. Eggplants are charred whole on a charcoal grill, then peeled, mashed and thickened with milk and cheese.

On this bed of rich creamy eggplant, tender morsels of slow-cooked beef are drizzled with the thin red gravy they were stewed in. The smoky taste from the grill lingers long after the immediate flavors from the stewpot have passed. It's the Beğendi experience that keeps us coming back for more.

Unfortunately, Hünkar Beğendi is only served at lunch, but the dinner menu has a few star attractions of its own. Among the meze tray standards, the stuffed artichoke heart dressed up with lemon and olive oil is a particularly tasty pick.

The Karaköy Salatası is a refreshing blast of greens spiked with beans. The thick yogurt in a small clay pot is irresistible as a side dish, or even as dessert.

On the hot side, the grilled octopus has the desired char to tenderness ratio. If you are as into innards as we are, you'll be happy to find a delicious hot starter of thinly sliced, lightly fried liver. If the catch of the day doesn't grab you, the lamb chops are sure not to disappoint. Traditional Turkish desserts like fruit compote, rice pudding and Aşure, a curious blend of fresh and dried fruits, nuts, wheat and rose water, are also on offer. ◆

Mutfak Dili
TRADESMEN'S PARADISE

Istanbul Eats' lunch hunting tips:
1) Wander into one of Istanbul's numerous districts of small tradesmen.
2) Enter one of these shops, preferably one where two old men are sitting at the counter looking at a horse racing form or working the crossword puzzle.
3) Ask them where they eat lunch. (Note: They might misinterpret your question and try to send you to the place they think you should eat lunch.) Repeat the question clearly: "Where do you eat lunch?"
4) Follow their directions to the nearest esnaf lokantası, or "tradesmen's restaurant."

This simple strategy is how we stumbled upon an excellent place called Mutfak Dili ("Kitchen Talk," in Turkish), a bustling lunch spot near the Golden Horn that keeps the local shop owners sated with cheap and tasty daily specials. For our starters we opted for the fresh stewed green beans served cold in olive oil and a bowl of Cacık, refreshing chilled yogurt with diced cucumbers. The İmambayıldı, eggplant stuffed with tomatoes peppers and onions and served cold, had perfect balance for a dish that usually seems to give way to the onions and garlic. The

126

Galata and the Docks

Tersane Caddesi, Ziyalı Sokak 10, Perşembe Pazarı, Karaköy
212 254 1154
8:30am-6pm; closed weekends

restaurant also serves esnaf lokantası classics like Patlıcan Karnıyarık, eggplant stuffed with meat and peppers, and Tas Kebabı, succulent beef stew.

For dessert, the Antep Fıstıklı Yeşil Yayla Tatlısı felt like the happy union of two of our favorite Turkish sweets, the syrup-soaked cake Revani and a traditional pistachio baklava. As we spooned the last of a

diabolical chocolate pudding called Aşkım Aşkım, one older tradesman walked by and eyed our table forlornly. "In the days when I could eat like that …"

Tradesmen do not have the luxury of traveling across the city at midday to fill their bellies. But for us, delicious food and a certain charm make Mutfak Dili well worth the trek. ◆

Çiğ Köfte
The Raw Deal

It may not quite be up there with Japan's fugu (blowfish meat that if prepared incorrectly can lead to death), but Turkey's çiğ köfte is one of those foods that carries with it a certain frisson of danger. Literally translated as "raw meatballs," the dish is made out of uncooked beef or lamb that is kneaded together with bulgur, tomato and pepper pastes, herbs and spices and then turned into small, oblong-shaped patties that are rolled up in a piece of crisp lettuce and eaten as appetizers. The taste of the uncooked meat paste, together with the cool lettuce, gives the dish a pleasant freshness.

A kind of Turkish steak tartare, çiğ köfte usually draws worried looks from visitors, concerned that ingesting raw meat might end up compromising their holiday plans.

We've been eating the stuff for years and have yet to experience an adverse reaction, but it would now appear that even Turks are starting to get skittish about eating raw meat. We've noticed an increasing number of çiğ köfte restaurants (some of them even part of chains specializing in the dish) open up around town, but almost all of them serving–sacré bleu!–meatless versions of the dish.

Still, the arrival of any culinary trend cannot be dismissed. So we present two spots, one serving classic çiğ köfte and the other the vegetarian variety, so readers can choose for themselves.

SUR OCAKBAŞI

Sur Ocakbaşı, a grill restaurant serving food from Turkey's southeast region, is located in Kadınlar Pazarı, a very pleasant pedestrian-only square in Istanbul's Fatih neighborhood. Çiğ köfte is a specialty of the region and, like at many restaurants there, the usta (or "master") who makes the stuff is accorded a place of honor. In Sur Ocakbaşı's case, the mustachioed usta has his own glass-lined booth, where he vigorously kneads the stuff. Being a çiğ köfte maker also apparently means being allowed to dress how you want. At Sur Ocakbaşı, the usta wears a shiny black suit, the sleeves of his jacket pushed up Miami Vice-style, in order to let him knead the meat with greater ease.

Along with the traditional lettuce wrap, Sur Ocakbaşı's köfte comes with a side of a dark, fiery pepper paste. It gives the tasty meatballs, which are already flavored with a dark, smoky dried pepper known as isot–an oily, almost black crushed red pepper from the southeastern Turkish city of Urfa–a very nice extra kick.

İtfaiye Caddesi 19,
Fatih
212 533 8088
10am-midnight

The streets of Beyoğlu's
Asmalımescit,
Tünel and Galata areas
no phone

HÜSEYİN'S
ÇİĞ KÖFTE
CART

Having one's hands stained red by pepper paste is an occupational hazard of the wandering çiğ köfte man. "Machine-made doesn't look like this," said Hüseyin Usta with the intensity of a misunderstood artist, thrusting up a freshly formed lump of çiğ köfte. Though taking its name from the raw meat appetizer, Hüseyin's çiğ köfte is a bulgur-based vegetarian creation. Aside from the crisp lettuce wrap, it is totally cooked, earning it the nickname "yalancı," or "liar's," çiğ köfte. Every day for the past 32 years, the no-nonsense Hüseyin has worked his secret mixture of bulgur, red pepper paste, parsley, onions and spices into moist little logs, tucking them away in his pushcart alongside lettuce, parsley and lavaş bread. Hüseyin's tender loving care is a hallmark of his çiğ köfte. But the key ingredient is a spicy paste made from isot. All that is good about this çiğ köfte–that smoky flavor, that creeping heat–is imparted by the isot.

Hüseyin pushes his cart through the streets of Beyoğlu every day selling his çiğ köfte wrapped in a leaf of crisp lettuce or rolled up in a flatbread. If you're in luck, you'll run across him–just be on the lookout for the man with the red pepper-stained hands.

Bosphorus

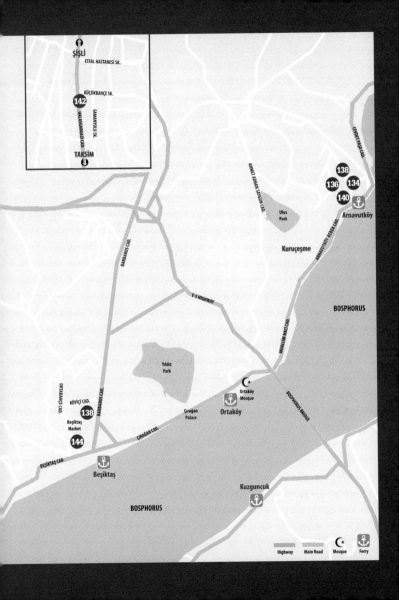

Satışmeydanı Sokak 2,
Arnavutköy
212 263 2933
noon-11pm

Adem Baba

SOLEMAN

Adem Baba, which got its start as a humble, boat-borne kitchen floating dockside in the Bosphorus neighborhood of Arnavutköy, is now a local seafood empire with three locations on the same street. Though the menu may resemble that of so many other Istanbul fish houses, consistent high quality and great value have earned the restaurant a cultish following.

On Sundays everyone is talking about the fish soup, which is so thick and aromatic it would make a New Englander swoon. Be forewarned: the soup is only served at Sunday lunch in the winter months. But even when there's no fish soup, the starters are never disappointing. Fried calamari is perfectly prepared–tender and crispy–and served with a tartar sauce à la Turca that smacks of garlic, walnuts and yogurt. The name Balık Köfte, fish balls, doesn't do justice to this Adem Baba special, a light and creamy bite of fish encased in a bat-

tered shell fried a deep brown. After the fried appetizers, cool down with a Kaşarlı Çoban Salatası, shepherd's salad with grated cheese, dressed with lemon and Adem Baba's fine olive oil.

Though you could easily make a full meal of appetizers and salad, it would be wrong to pass on the fish course. Particularly in winter, the region's finest and freshest fish are on offer. Grilled sardalya, a sardine of sorts, hides a tender salty zing within its charred crunchy skin. A plate of grilled or fried dil balığı (sole) is a fine choice not available at most restaurants. Thick flaky cuts of grilled dülger, John Dory fish, appear on the menu regularly and are also not to be missed. But when Black Sea anchovies, hamsi, are in season and served fried in a cornmeal batter, we have little willpower to resist them. Although Adem Baba has no wine list, it remains one of our favorite dry lunches and is quite affordable as well. ◆

1. Cadde 111,
Arnavutköy
212 263 2918
open 24 hours

Bodrum Mantı

SUPERMANTI

From Western China all the way to Istanbul, Turkic people roll out dough, fold it into small pouches, boil it and call it mantı. When it comes to dumplings, Turkish tradition dictates that the tortellini-like mantı be no larger than peanut-sized. With its unusually large (and sometimes fried) dumplings, Bodrum Mantı & Café has taken traditional Turkish mantı to soaring new heights, of which we strongly approve.

Don't be put off by the modish décor, the dour bow-tied waiters or the high street address; this is the real article. This 24-hour Arnavutköy staple with a Bosphorus view never fails to serve it up hot, fast, good and cheap.

The İçli Köfte–football-shaped patties of ground meat encased in boiled or fried bulgur–is always made to order, unlike many oil-soaked renditions found around town.

Stick a fork in the Çiğ Börek and watch–or, better yet, smell–the hot airy pocket pastry deflate in an aromatic whoosh, revealing a light filling of ground meat. Like the mantı, these appetizers come jumbo, so be forewarned.

The mantı is offered in a few varieties: whole wheat or white dough, boiled or fried. We couldn't discern the wheat from the white dough when fried, but in boiled form the whole wheat offered a pleasant change. Ordering half portions allowed us to try many combinations of fillings and toppings.

The pièce de résistance, Temel Feriye Mantı, is fried just enough for the thin shell to crisp up and the stuffing of spinach, onions and cheese to meld nicely without being greasy. This mantı even holds up well under a generous topping of garlic yogurt sauce. Supermantı, indeed. ◆

136

Can Ciğer

FOR THE LIVER LOVER IN YOU

Turkey's passionate love affair with liver can turn downright obsessive in some parts of the country. The city of Edirne, filled with restaurants selling the dish and nothing but, is perhaps ground zero for Turkish liver lovers. Indeed, for many Turks, the name Edirne is simply synonymous with liver. We visited the city several years ago and had what was a very fine plate of liver done in the local style. Although we're not liver-crazy enough to make the drive there just to eat the stuff (as some Istanbulites do), we were very happy to discover Can Ciğer, a small spot in Beşiktaş that's one of the few places in Istanbul serving up Edirne-style liver.

The formula for making the dish is simple: extremely fresh cow's liver is sliced into very thin, almost bite-size pieces, coated with flour and then deep-fried until crisp and approaching something that could be described as Liver

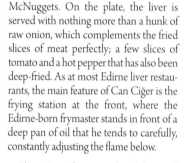

McNuggets. On the plate, the liver is served with nothing more than a hunk of raw onion, which complements the fried slices of meat perfectly; a few slices of tomato and a hot pepper that has also been deep-fried. As at most Edirne liver restaurants, the main feature of Can Ciğer is the frying station at the front, where the Edirne-born frymaster stands in front of a deep pan of oil that he tends to carefully, constantly adjusting the flame below.

The attention he pays to the oil shows off in the liver. On our visit, the meat was perfectly fried and–perhaps because of its thinness and crispy coating–had none of the "livery" taste we usually associate with the dish. Sitting around us, meanwhile, were local liver freaks, some who had even ordered a double portion of the crispy nuggets, clearly happy that instead of having to go to Edirne to get their fix, Edirne had come to them. ◆

Fıstık Kebap

MUCH LOVE FOR LAHMACUN

Let's face it: lahmacun is easy to get excited about. It checks all of the boxes of a perfect savory snack: crispy oven-fired crust, light and spicy meat spread, with a fresh green topping and a tangy spray from a lemon. It's like an artisanal pizza with a Middle Eastern topping wrapped around a side salad–for the cost of a shoeshine. How anyone could not love lahmacun is beyond us. Still, we hear they are out there. The only explanation is that they never had a really good one, meaning they never set foot in Fıstık Kebap, the be-all and end-all of lahmacun in Istanbul.

Located on the Bosphorus in the upmarket district of Arnavutköy, Fıstık has no use for the pretensions that its address may indicate. This is a down and dirty neighborhood kebab joint with a small seating area and a bustling delivery business. Ac-

cording to the overworked man at the oven, İbrahim Usta, more than 500 lahmacun pass over his paddle every day. Fıstık also serves the usual kebab selection–Adana, Urfa, chicken–but the main attraction here is the lahmacun.

We challenge those not so hot on lahmacun to resist oohing and ahhing as İbrahim Usta slides his paddle into the oven and fetches out a fresh one. The brick oven's rage renders the crust a bubbled, crispy fantasy–charred here, still soft and pulsing like a soufflé there.

He'll roll it into a wrap if you like or quarter it before plating it with a small salad for dressing. With a cold glass of şalgam, or fermented turnip juice, this quick bite is the perfect segue from lunch to dinner, or dinner to breakfast. İbrahim mans the oven until midnight. ◆

Kaburga Sofrası

THE RIB SHACK

In eastern Turkey, a lamb is consumed literally from head to tail, with hardly any part of the animal going uncooked. One of the specialties of the region, particularly in the area around the picturesque city of Mardin, is kaburga–breast of lamb–a cut akin to short ribs that often ends up in the scrap heap in other parts of the world.

At Kaburga Sofrası, kaburga is given the royal treatment, stuffed with peppery rice and slow-cooked for some eight hours, until the meat turns meltingly tender. It's presented with a flourish: a waiter brings it to the table on a large platter covered with a silver dome, delivering it to another waiter, who then takes over, deboning the steaming, tender meat and shredding it into bite-size morsels.

Along with the flavorful İç Pilav–the rice that was stuffed and cooked inside the ribs–the kaburga is served with a side of rice mixed with fresh parsley and roasted almonds, offering a crunchy contrast to the soft meat. Of course, lamb also appears in other forms on the menu, such as in the İçli Köfte, ground meat, sautéed onion, parsley and spices that are stuffed into a bulgur wheat shell and then poached to make a very large and tasty dumpling.

Mumbar, another specialty from the Mardin area, is lamb intestine stuffed with ground meat, rice and mint (and frankly, something whose rubbery funk we've never warmed up to, as much as we've tried). In the excellent and earthy Güveç, cubes of lamb, eggplant, tomatoes and green pepper are slowly cooked in a clay pot until all of the ingredients become soft as butter and almost meld together.

To make things easy, dessert is limited to one choice: İrmik Helvası, or sweetened semolina studded with pine nuts and served warm. It's quite tasty, but chances are that by this point you'll be feeling as stuffed as, well, a lamb. ◆

142

Kaymak:
The Heavenly Cream

In our imagination, kaymak, the delicious Turkish version of clotted cream, is the only food served in heaven, where angels in white robes dish out plate after plate of the cloudlike stuff to the dearly departed, who no longer have to worry about cholesterol counts and visits to the cardiologist. Perhaps we're getting carried away, but kaymak can do that to you. For our money, the classic Turkish "bal-kaymak" combo, or kaymak served under a blanket of honey with crusty white bread, is one of the finest breakfasts anywhere.

The stuff is glorious, but simple. Milk, preferably from domesticated water buffaloes known as "manda" in Turkish, is slowly boiled until a thick layer of very rich, pure white cream forms at the top. After it cools, the kaymak is rolled up into little logs that have a consistency that hovers somewhere in between liquid and solid, with a creamy taste that's both subtle and rich at the same time. The stuff is also quite delicate, with a shelf life of barely one day. Still, purists refuse to refrigerate it, lest it lose its texture and pick up any refrigerator odors. Like we said, kaymak can make people get carried away.

Three of our favorite places to try kaymak are:

BEŞİKTAŞ KAYMAKÇI

This tiny shop/eatery has been in business since 1895 and it certainly shows its age. The marble counter is cracked and the paint on the walls peeling. But the kaymak, served up by 84-year-old Pando, a living institution in Istanbul's untouristy Beşiktaş bazaar, is out of this world. Prices here also seem unchanged since 1895: a plate of kaymak and honey, served with fresh bread and a glass of steaming hot milk, will set you back just a few lira.

Mumcu Bakkal Sokak 5,
Beşiktaş
212 258 2616
8am-7pm

BORİS'İN YERİ

Ördekli Bakkal Sokak 17,
Kumkapı
212 517 2256
6:30am-10:30pm

Boris'in Yeri ("Boris's Place") has been keeping Kumkapı's restaurants and residents stocked with bal-kay-mak for almost a century. And from the looks of the place, little has changed since Boris first set up shop. Old cracked tile floors, marble tables worn from use and a pair of stain-less steel coolers the size of Buicks are about the only decor you'll find here.

KARAKÖY ÖZSÜT

Compared to Pando's place in Beşiktaş, this place, open since 1915, is a relative newcomer to the kaymak scene. Located near the Karaköy waterfront, Özsüt serves up very good kaymak (as well as yogurt and rustic cheeses) made from the restaurant's own herd of water buffaloes, whose pictures grace the walls.

Yemişçi Hasan Sokak 9/11, Karaköy
212 293 3031
5am-6pm

Asian Side and Islands

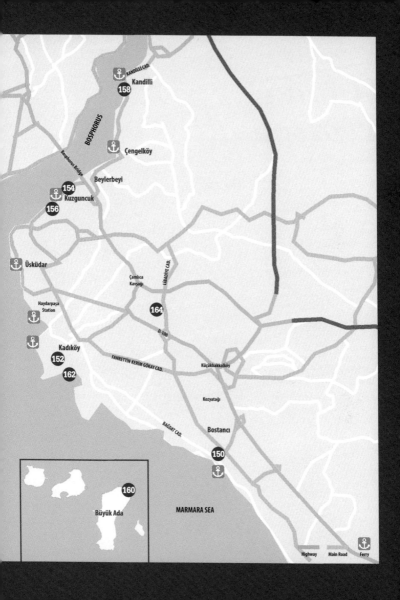

Bağdat Caddesi 535/A,
Alt Bostancı
216 380 1710
11am-11pm

Adana Özasmaaltı

CLUB KEBAB

At Adana Özasmaaltı on the waterfront in Bostancı, there's no poring over a labyrinthine menu and no anxiety about what to order. Folks come here to eat Adana Kebap, the spicy ground lamb kebab named for a city in the south of Turkey, and they come often. Regulars know the waiter's name and he knows how they drink their rakı. With its walls lined with photographs and the tiny vine-laden terrace upstairs, the place feels like a local clubhouse. In Istanbul, it's not easy for a kebab place to stand out in the crowd, as Adana Özasmaaltı does. What's their secret? As the grill man explained, "For 35 years we've been making Adana Kebap from good, hand-cut meat, with sumac and onions on the side and fresh lavaş. That's the way it's done in Adana, so that's how we do it." As simple as that sounds, the result is unusually complex and quite different from most Adana kebabs in Istanbul. After a quick palate cleanser of sharp, arugula-like greens and cool, white slices of radish to start things off, the kebab arrived at the table still sizzling. It was three fingers wide and nearly too long for the plate.

The paper-thin lavaş underneath had already started to disintegrate where the kebab's juices gathered. The skin of the quartered and grilled tomato that came with the meat had split and blackened. On the side sat a beautiful plate of lilac-colored onions spiked with sumac.

We went to work, laying down a trail of onions on some lavaş and topping them with grilled pepper and then the Adana, which almost crumbled with the nudge of a fork. The tang of the onions hit first, opening the way for the smoky heat of the red pepper-riddled Adana, in which the quality of the meat came through along with its textural subtleties. And that rich flavor? A little fat from the tail of the lamb. After all, that's the way it's done in Adana. ◆

Çiya

LOQUAT KEBABS AND MESOPOTAMIAN TRUFFLES AT ISTANBUL'S CULINARY SHRINE

The Asian-side eatery Çiya Sofrası is very likely the best restaurant in Istanbul. Thanks to glowing write-ups in numerous places, Çiya is no longer the off-the-beaten-path secret it once was, but the restaurant has remained true to what made it successful in the first place. That success comes from the vision of owner-chef Musa Dağdeviren, who hails from the southeastern Turkish city of Gaziantep and who is something of a culinary anthropologist, collecting recipes from around Turkey. The result is a menu

that features unusual regional dishes that you will very likely not find anywhere else. What's on offer changes daily, which means there isn't an actual menu. Instead, ordering is done by walking up to a chef who watches over more than a dozen bubbling pots and other dishes containing prepared food and pointing to what looks interesting.

The day's "menu," which always features a variety of vegetarian dishes, changes according to what's in season. On one visit we ate a delicious meat stew cooked with brac-

ingly tart unripe green plums, as well as keme, a mushroom found in Anatolia that we like to think of as a Mesopotamian truffle. Cut up in slices and grilled on a skewer, this hearty fungus tastes like an earthy cross between a Portobello mushroom and a very delicate potato. Springtime specials include Yeni Dünya Kebap, which is made out of pitted loquats that are stuffed with ground meat and then grilled, as well as artichokes stuffed with rice and herbs. On another visit, we had very tasty and unusual dolma (stuffed grape leaves) which were filled with rice and lor, a kind of farmer's cheese, and topped with caramelized onions. Çiya isn't the fanciest or most "cutting-edge" place in town, but we rarely leave without having a profoundly new and memorable taste experience. ◆

153

Arabacılar Sok. No:4,
Beylerbeyi
216-557-6686

Inciralti
Meyhane Time Machine

We like to think of Inciralti, a laid back meyhane in the sleepy Bosphorus-side Beylerbeyi neighborhood, as a destination restaurant – not so much because of the food, but because of the destination itself.

Not that there's anything wrong with the food, which is reliably well made. The meze tray is brought to your table carrying all the classics, plus a few welcome and tasty surprises, such as the zingy brined twigs of the caper plant and a sea bass filet that had been cured in a piquant sauce redolent of curry. Among our excellent mains, we had sea bass again, this time grilled wrapped inside grape vine leaves, and meltingly soft grilled uykuluk (sweetbreads). Both were winners.

But it's Inciralti's location that will have us coming back, especially if we're looking for an opportunity to take an excursion without leaving Istanbul. Located on the Asian side, Beylerbeyi is a like a miniature and untouristed version of the European side's more popular Ortakoy area, mercifully free of the vendors and crowds that today line that neighborhood's streets. Stepping off the evening ferry at Beylerbeyi's old wooden one-room ferry terminal feels a bit like stepping back in time. There are few Bosphorus-side neighborhoods that have managed to keep their unpretentious original charm they way this one has.

Inciralti (the name means "under the fig tree") is located inside a welcoming old house on a small side street a few steps away from the ferry terminal. In the back there's a leafy garden (home to the restaurant's namesake fig tree) that, like Beylerbeyi itself, has a transporting quality to it ◆

(Note: to reach Beylerbeyi, take the Bosphorus commuter ferry that leaves from Eminonu. Check the schedule here: www.ido.com.tr)

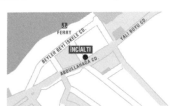

Çarşı Caddesi 1/A,
Kuzguncuk
216 553 1232
noon-midnight

İsmet Baba

GREAT FISH FOR GOODFELLAS

Diners in Istanbul are spoiled with options for fresh seafood. But most restaurants are mere caricatures of places like İsmet Baba, where traditions have been kept sacred for more than 50 years. Located in Kuzguncuk, a charming neighborhood on the Asian side of the Bosphorus, it may not be the city's best restaurant, but it's got something most of the others have lost, old-school Istanbul charm and character.

At İsmet Baba, we like to lean back, hunker down into a long rakı-laced dinner and really enjoy this special place. We start with the meze tray. Alas, it only takes a few meals out in Istanbul to memorize most of its offerings, and İsmet Baba isn't carrying any wild cards. However, the Pilaki, beans in olive oil, and the cold octopus salad are unusually good. We also like the Haydari, a thick, tangy spread of strained yogurt and dill, and the fried eggplant with a garlicky yogurt drizzle. Slices of Lakerda, pickled tunny, are a must for many; on one visit, we ordered a second portion of this sashimi-like appetizer. Cold sheep brains are not our favorite meze, but at İsmet Baba you can have them fried up as a smart little tempura-like dish, alongside calamari and a house specialty börek filled with spinach and potatoes.

The catch of the day and its price per portion are posted on a small blackboard in the dining room. The fried kalkan (turbot) can be a bit heavy after so many rounds of starters. We found the çipura (grilled bream) and a plate of çinekop (bluefish) perfectly prepared and just the right amount. After the bottle is empty, and you've had your fill of Turkish coffee, don't forget to nod goodbye to the old codgers at the VIP table drinking to İsmet Baba and days long gone; they'll keep an eye on the place, making sure nothing changes while you're gone. ◆

Kandilli İskele Caddesi 4-17,
Üsküdar
216 332 3241
10am-12am

Kandilli Suna'nın Yeri

PORT OF CALL

One afternoon at Suna'nın Yeri, a small fish restaurant on the Bosphorus waterfront of the Kandilli neighborhood, a small boat with the name "Guernsey" pulled up and unloaded two hungry passengers. We wouldn't be surprised if the couple had actually come all the way from that island in the British Channel–the food at Suna'nın Yeri ("Suna's Place," in Turkish) is just that good.

The chilled fava bean puree was so delicious that we immediately ordered two more. Though it's usually not our first pick from the meze tray, Suna had coaxed something smooth and rich, almost custard-like out of the humble fava without abandoning its earthy beany flavor. A plate of fried calamari was also a pleasant surprise: rough bundles of crispy legs and tiny rings were mixed with large, soft flat pieces and each bite was a new chapter in texture, accompanied by a delicious, tangy garlic sauce.

We relished this rare moment–perfectly prepared, fresh food served in an environment celebrating nothing more than the inherent beauty of Istanbul itself–feeling that this was what a dining experience was inherently supposed to be.

Though big catches such as levrek (sea bass), çipura (sea bream) and kalkan (turbot) were tempting, we took our cue from the tables around us and ordered a large plate of small fried fish: hamsi (anchovies), flayed and ribbon-like; istavrit (mackerel); and our favorite, tekir (mullet). Each fish played its part with ease, as if Suna had had a pep talk with the group before frying them in her kitchen. After all that fish and a few rounds of "special cola" (cans of Efes Dark beer delivered with a wink in a plastic bag and served in Coca-Cola glasses), we wanted more. We soon found ourselves swooning over a plate of homemade baklava.

We'll carry that sweet memory with us until our next visit. ◆

Çiçekli Yalı Sokak 2,
Büyükada
216 382 5606
8:30am-midnight

Kıyı

A WINNING ISLAND CASTAWAY

On Büyükada, the largest of the Princes' Islands, we had always found the dining scene disappointing. The row of busy fish restaurants beside the ferry terminal all have similar, predictable menus and serve up equal amounts of hustle. Kıyı, however, is an antidote to all this, a wonderful restaurant that puts its competitors to shame. While its rivals have impressive waterfront terraces, Kıyı's is a charming, ramshackle affair, shaded by creeping vines and looking like it's about to topple over into the sea.

But the biggest difference is in the kitchen. Kıyı's extensive meze menu includes some unusual and very tasty items, particularly a quartet of extremely fresh salads made with greens and lettuces grown on the island by Kıyı's owner, Adnan, and a trio of meze made from wild greens that are found in salty marshes near the sea. We particularly liked the Deniz Fasulyesi ("sea bean"), a mellow green that looked a bit like rosemary and which was stewed with garlic in olive oil and served cold. Another standout was a ceviche made out of locally-caught iskorpit (scorpion fish). Among the hot appetizers, Kıyı's unusual Rum Börek ("Greek börek"), a slice of eggplant topped with a spread made out of farmer's cheese and dill and then fried, was something we'd never seen before.

The restaurant has a fairly large–if not obscure–selection of fish every day. On our visit, along with the levrek (sea bass) and istavrit (mackerel) that you find everywhere else, the case also held a large, glistening mercan (common pandora), a catfish-like kırlangıç (grey gurnard) and dülger (John Dory). Kıyı grills most of its fish, but we were pulled by the barbunya (red mullet), which are served fried in a light dusting of flour. Of course, the most appealing catch of all is Kıyı itself. ◆

Moda Caddesi 265,
Moda
216 336 0795
noon-midnight

Koço

QUEST FOR THE HOLY GRILL

Reviewers are often tempted into using metaphors that portray the restaurant as a sacred place: a sushi temple, a T-bone pilgrimage, chili-cheese-fry heaven. But in Istanbul's Moda district on the Asian shore, we've found a praise-worthy fish restaurant that could justifiably be described as a shrine—literally. For more than 50 years, a local Greek family has been serving saints and sinners alike at Koço, a rambling seaside fish house situated atop an ayazma, or sacred spring. There's meze and fresh grilled fish with rakı upstairs, candles and holy water downstairs.

We couldn't resist the octopus salad recommended by the waiter, and tender it was, sitting in a drizzle of olive oil alongside chopped pickles. If the quality of an octopus is decided by its tenderness, smoke is the factor in Patlıcan Salatası, or eggplant puree. A good dish of this lovely spread should not only

smell and taste of the grill but give the impression that it's been down there socializing with the charcoal for days, as Koço's did. Cibes, a large leafy Brussels sprout-like vegetable, was the meze tray wild card. Cool, soft and pleasantly coated in garlicky olive oil, this was unlike any Brussels sprouts we've had.

But the real pleasure of the meal was a perfectly grilled lüfer, or bluefish. Our fish was so moist and tasty it almost seemed as if it had been doused in butter. But no, it was just a very fresh fish in the hands of a grill man with a lot of practice and the power of prayer behind him. Clearly, whatever blessings being recited down in the basement must have passed through the grill on their way up to the heavens.

A full spread at Koço with local wine or rakı is quite affordable. A small donation for a candle downstairs in the shrine is optional. ◆

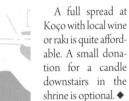

Beans:
An Investigative Report

Until we visited some of Istanbul's shrines to the baked bean, we generally regarded the dish as something eaten out of a can beside railroad tracks. But Turkey takes this humble food seriously; that means chefs in tall toques carefully ladling out golden beans in a rich red gravy onto monogrammed flatware, served by waiters wearing bowties and vests. Even in the least formal of Istanbul's beaneries, the guy manning the pot has the air of a high priest knowing that his incantations alone conjure something unusually delicious out of a simple dry white legume. This is no hobo fare.

There are two general schools of bean cooking in Turkey: Black Sea and Anatolian. Beans Black Sea-style sit in a red gravy so thick with butter and laden with chunks of meat that we eat it with a fork and a hearty piece of bread. Anatolian beans, often known as Erzincan beans, are soupier and cooked in a tomato-based sauce without butter and meat. Either way, you can't go wrong.

The following are three of our favorite bean joints in town:

FASULİ LOKANTASI

The beans at Fasuli Lokantası glow unbelievably orange, as if the chef slipped a little something radioactive in the pot. Whatever the recipe, these beans are among the best we've had in Istanbul. Stiffened by a whole lot of butter, the gravy and beans almost achieve the same creamy consistency. The cool, crisp raw onions and pickled hot peppers are a welcome balance to the richness of the dish, although their aroma stays with you long after your meal. Host to a loyal lunch crowd, this white-tablecloth establishment serves up other Black Sea specialties including Muhlama, a sort of Turkish fondue; stuffed chard leaves, and corn bread. The location, across the street from Tophane's nargile cafes and near the Karaköy waterfront, is an added bonus.

İskele Caddesi 10-12,
Tophane
212 243 6580
11am-11pm

Erzincanlı Ali Baba

ERZİNCANLI ALİ BABA

According to historians, Tiryaki Sokak–Addicts Alley–got its name from the opium served up in its coffeehouses during Ottoman times. Though that substance has been long banned, since 1924 Ali Baba has been ladling out something equally addictive from a great copper pot: Erzincan-style baked beans. Ingredients such as onion, tomato and chili pepper are more recognizable in the soupy base, the bean bigger than its Black Sea counterpart. Though we remain junkies of the Black Sea variety, the Erzincan preparation is a nice change of pace and there's no better place to try a bowl than sitting on Ali Baba's squat stools in the shadow of the minarets of the sublime Süleymaniye mosque.

Prof. Sıddık Sami Onar Caddesi 11, Süleymaniye
212 513 6219
noon-8:30pm

ÇÖMLEK

At Çömlek you can't miss the huge red clay cauldron sitting behind the counter. The fellow with the big ladle says it's the pot that makes these beans better than the rest. Cooking vessel aside, a serving of these beans also has the highest meat count of any place we've visited in Istanbul. Whereas most beans might have a shred or at best a few nuggets of tender roasted beef in there for flavor, Çömlek's are crowned by generous helping of meat. In such a rich dish the meat satisfyingly offsets the cloying beans, leaving the meek still able to walk away and the strong-willed able order up another half-portion. The restaurant, located on the wooded slopes above Üsküdar on the Asian side, is a bit out of the way. But for us, these are beans at their best and worth the trip.

Turistik Çamlıca Caddesi 50, Çamlıca
216 316 2953
11am-11pm

Glossary

domates konuşmaz.
Çünkü bu domatesi yedi...

Index

Glossary

acı: *hot or bitter*

armut: *pear*

aşçı: *cook*

ayran: *a drink of beaten yogurt, cold water and salt*

az pişmiş: *rare*

az şekerli: *slightly sweet*

badem: *almond*

baharat: *spices*

bal: *honey*

balık: *fish*

bardak: *drinking glass*

beyaz: *white, as in white beans*

beyaz şarap: *white wine*

biber: *pepper*

biftek: *beefsteak*

bira: *beer*

börek: *filled pastries in various shapes, baked, fried, or grilled*

buz: *ice*

cacık: *grated cucumber in yogurt with garlic and dill*

ceviz: *walnut*

ciğer: *liver*

çay: *tea*

çiğ: *raw*

çilek: *strawberry*

çorba: *soup*

dereotu: *dill*

dolma: *stuffed vegetable*

domates: *tomato*

dondurma: *ice cream*

ekmek: *bread*

ekşi: *sour*

elma: *apple*

erik: *plum*

esnaf lokantası: *tradesmen's restaurant*

et: *meat*

fasulye: *bean*

fındık: *hazelnut*

fincan: *cup*

gül: *rose*

güveç: *earthenware casserole*

havuç: *carrot*

helva: *sesame paste dessert*

incir: *fig*

kadayıf: *finely shredded pastry used to make a dessert*

kahvaltı: *breakfast*

kahve: *coffee*

kara biber: *black pepper*

karanfil: *clove*

karides: *shrimp*

karnıbahar: *cauliflower*

karpuz: *watermelon*

kavun: *melon*

kavurma: *cubed and braised lamb for stews*

kayısı: *apricot*

kaymak: *clotted cream*

kekik: *thyme*

kızartma: *browned in oil*

köfte: *Turkish meatballs*

közleme: *grilled*

kuru: *dried*

kuzu: *lamb*

leblebi: *roasted and dried chickpeas*

limon: *lemon*

lokanta: *restaurant*

lokum: *Turkish delight*

mantar: *mushroom*

mantı: *small pasta purses filled with minced meat, similar to ravioli*

maydanoz: *parsley*

meyve: *fruit*

mısır: *corn*

mutfak: *kitchen or cuisine*

muz: *banana*

nane: *mint*

nar: *pomegranate*

orta: *medium, as in medium-sweet coffee*

orta şekerli: *medium-sweet, as in sweetened coffee*

pancar: *beet*

pastırma: *spiced sun-dried beef*

pazar: *market*

pekmez: *grape molasses*

peynir: *cheese*

pide: *a flat, oval bread served plain, or meat filled*

pilaki: *a bean dish cooked in olive oil, served cold*

piyaz: *bean salad, served cold*

reçel: *jam*

sakız: *the resin from the mastic tree*

sarımsak: *garlic*

sarma: *wrapped leaves of grape, or cabbage, filled with minced meat or rice*

sıcak: *hot*

soğuk: *cold*

sucuk: *a preserved meat "sausage" of lamb and beef*

sulu yemek: *home cooking*

süt: *milk*

şarap: *wine*

şeftali: *peach*

şeker: *sugar*

şişe: *bottle*

tatlı: *sweet, or desserts, in general*

tava: *fried*

taze: *fresh*

tuz: *salt*

un: *flour*

üzüm: *grape*

yarım porsiyon: *half a regular-sized portion*

yeşil: *green, as in green peppers*

yumurta: *egg*

zeytin: *olive*

zeytinyağı: *olive oil*

FISH

barbunya/barbun: *red mullet/striped mullet*

çipura: *gilthead seabream*

dil: *common sole*

dülger: *John Dory*

fener: *angler/anglerfish*

hamsi: *anchovy*

istavrit: *Atlantic horse mackerel*

kalkan: *turbot*

kırlangıç: *grey gurnard*

lagos: *white grouper*

levrek: *sea bass*

lüfer: *bluefish*

mercan: *common seabream*

mezgit: *whiting*

palamut: *Atlantic bonito*

sardalya: *sardine*

tekir: *striped red mullet*

uskumru: *Atlantic mackerel*

Index

Alphabetically

Vegetarian-friendly